LITURGY: ACTIVE PARTICIPATION
IN THE DIVINE LIFE

Father Fred Barr

We are Catholics because we have
been chosen!
participation p. 46 NB

LITURGY: ACTIVE PARTICIPATION IN THE DIVINE LIFE
Where We've Been—Where We're Going

Major Addresses from the
1989 National Meeting
of the Diocesan Liturgical Commissions

*Jointly sponsored by the
Federation of Diocesan Liturgical Commissions
and the
Bishops' Committee on the Liturgy*

Fred Moleck
Marchita B. Mauck
Mark Searle
Irene Nowell, O.S.B.
Rembert G. Weakland, O.S.B.

Editor: James P. Moroney

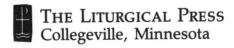
THE LITURGICAL PRESS
Collegeville, Minnesota

Cover design by MARY JO PAULY

Contents

Foreword

JAMES P. MORONEY

When I was a little boy, old Mrs. Kelly used to come to church every day. She knelt enthusiastically on creaking kneelers (or was that her knees?) and clutched her beads like they were God himself come to hear her prayers. Occasionally and most notably when the altar boy rang the bells, she would gaze far away "up there" at a man holding a little white host in which seemed to reside her whole reality, her whole reason for being. I remember watching her come back from Communion, head bowed and deeply drawn inside herself. There was something awesome and wonderful about Mrs. Kelly, about her God, and about what they were doing together at Mass.

Mrs. Kelly has been dead now for many years. So too, despite some minor appearances, is the rite she used to participate in. But the liturgy goes on, as it did in Hippolytus' Rome, Caesarius' Aries, and Luther's Germany. Mrs. Kelly still participates in the sacrifice of the altar, the heavenly banquet of the Lamb.

We have been trying, as of late, to help people to participate in the liturgy. "Like the response to a litany,"[1] the

1. Herman Schmidt, S.J., *La Constitution de la Sainte Liturgie* (Brussels: Editions Lumen Vitae, 1966) 204.

7

word "participation" (*participare, participatio*) recurs twenty-six times in The Constitution on the Sacred Liturgy. Indeed, the council Fathers told us, participation is "the aim to be considered before all else" in the liturgical reform.

This slim tome contains the reflections of five people, brought together some twenty-five years after the writing of those words to reflect on how well we have understood them. The group which brought them together consists of representatives of all diocesan liturgical commissions and offices in the United States, gathered for the annual National Meeting of Diocesan Liturgical Commissions. The meeting at which these papers were delivered, held in Pittsburgh in October of 1989, was jointly sponsored by the Federation of Diocesan Liturgical Commissions and the Bishops' Committee on the Liturgy.

The talks were presented by a liturgist, a Scripture scholar, a liturgical musician, an anthropologist, and an archbishop. Each of them seeks to define participation, but more importantly, each tries to help us to be participants in Christ's worship of the Father in the liturgy.

Mark Searle calls for nothing short of a relaunching of the liturgical movement. While describing an unconscious enculturation which the liturgy undergoes in each parish, he warns that such accomodation is not so much a matter of squeezing the liturgy into culture as inserting our lives into Christ. Participation is first participation in God's life and then participation through Christ in "the worship that all creation owes to God." Searle challenges us to transcend parochial conceptions of liturgical practice, go beyond our stereotypes of God, and shift the focus of attention from us to God.

Sr. Irene Nowell shows us how the natural connections

of community and worship in the Old Testament are just as true for our assemblies today. From covenant to community to communal worship, we must demand and create community in what may be the most countercultural action we take in an age of individualists!

Fred Moleck conducts a nostalgic pilgrimage through the struggles to accept and embrace our "indispensable roles in singing the song of the body of Christ." I find myself humming the tunes of songs I'd rather forget I sang (or led!), while Moleck's reflections give us the perspective which only retrospect can provide.

Marchita Mauck gives us some "home movies" with an anthropological focus on our liturgical adolescence. By remembering where we used to put the furniture (altar, presider's chair, tabernacle, banners, statues, and fonts) and the people (commentator, assembly), she teaches us to discover some unique and often startling meanings behind our notions of participation.

Finally, Archbishop Weakland gives us a wholistic vision of liturgy as a bridge between altar, pulpit, faith community, and marketplace. His talk is filled with practical applications and observations concerning everything from the risks of "our intense accentuation of the human" to pressing questions in liturgical music, art, wedding liturgies, and general intercessions.

All of these talks and all of the people who listened to them are devoted to encouraging the "Mrs. Kellys" of today to make themselves one with the timeless mystery which is worship. In their voices we hear Augustine's reminder that God wants us more than our gifts[2] and Gregory the Great's

2. Augustine, *Sermon* 82.5.

admonition that "the mass will be a sacrifice for us only when we have made an offering of ourselves to God."[3] From the earliest days of the Church's life we have been cajoled, encouraged, and reminded that the goal to be considered before all else is that full and active participation which is demanded by the very nature of the liturgy. May we have the good faith and good sense to listen.

3. Gregory the Great, *Dialogues* 4.59.

In the restoration and promotion of the sacred liturgy the full and active participation by all the people is the aim to be considered before all else, for it is the primary and indispensable source from which the faithful are to derive the true Christian spirit. Therefore, in all their apostolic activity, pastors of souls should energetically set about achieving it through the requisite pedagogy.

The Constitution on the Sacred Liturgy, no. 14

Music

FRED MOLECK

There were not many places in the preconciliar days that boasted a developed and effective music ministry. There were elements, however, that appear to have been universal to the majority of American parishes, as they fulfilled the canon to have some musical expression of the Roman rite. Usually it was the daily schedule of morning Masses, whose legislation demanded that those Masses be sung in order to fulfill the requirement of the High Mass and its stipend, but it included also the midweek novena and Benediction with the ubiquitous "O Salutaris Hostia" and "Tantum Ergo." The music ministry in those parishes was usually fufilled by the organist, who played and sang in the west gallery at both early morning times and early evening times. Most of the parishioners didn't know the organist's name, but the same parishioners knew the name of the janitor, the school principal, the pastor (maybe), and the new curate (only if their children were in the CYO). The Sunday-morning ministry was most developed with a parish choir, who sang at the High Mass that frequently had Benediction after it; there was a 9:00 A.M. school Mass at which the children might sing; and, in some places, Vespers and Benediction on Sunday afternoon. (The quality of the repertory and its performance is outside the scope of this paper.) Most Catholics knew "O Salutaris Hostia," "Tantum Ergo," "Bring

13

Flowers of the Fairest," and "Holy God, We Praise Thy Name." Other than that, the repertory was determined by geography and the ethnic origins of the parish.

There were rumblings about active participation in some parishes and even in some dioceses. Hymns designed to fit the parts of the Mass in the manner of the German *Sing-messe*, dialogue Masses, and the appearance of Collegeville's little green book, *Our Parish Prays and Sings* (The Liturgical Press, 1966), were the first signs of change in the parish's worship program. With the ammunition provided by Msgr. Martin Hellriegel of St. Louis, experimentations in active participation were conducted in many parts of the Mid-western United States, though numerous parishes and dioceses were unaware of the nearly one-hundred-year history of liturgical research, ritual experimentation, and the development of the priesthood of the faithful. Most music programs expressed the model of liturgy that retained the solo voice, the solo choir, the solo source of musical participation. When the premier document of Vatican II declared "full, active and conscious participation of all the faithful" (The Constitution on the Sacred Liturgy, no. 14), well, what a shock! We were all to sing. But what were we to sing? German and Polish and Slovak and Middle European parishes had been singing things for quite a while. But what of the territorial parish?

The first solution extracted hymns and replanted them where they could do the least harm—at the beginning and the end and twice in between. Two solutions were "Praise to the Lord" and "Lord, Accept the Gifts We Offer." Hymnals, hymn cards, and missalettes were everywhere. Service music tended to be conservative in the sense that the music was a chant *adaptatio* or a new setting of the text in very

straight, traditional harmonies and melodic writing. Jan
Vermulst's *Mass for Christian Unity* was everywhere. It was
Alexander Peloquin who dared to break out of a *musica sacra*
mold. Peloquin utilized 6/8 patterns in his "Gloria of the
Bells" and his *Missa a la Samba.* Clarence Rivers success-
fully wedded the blues harmonies of flatted sevenths and
thirds to the liturgical texts of his *American Mass.* "God Is
Love" is his most memorable.

As the experimentations continued, the Church continued to define itself. Some thought that a new musical and
textual language was needed. Some thought that this innova-
tive use of contemporary harmonies would be especially relevant to the younger members of the Church. Joe Wise, Jack
Miffleton, Tom Parker, and certainly Ray Repp tilled the
first soil from which would spring a folk style that is very
much a part of our worship language today. The previous
generation's contribution to Catholic youth music was "Banner of Truth," etc., which now exists as a quaint reminder
of our triumphalistic notion of the Church on the march.
It was a miraculous jump to make from that battle song to
"Kumbyah," Ray Repp's "Sons of God," and Sr. Miriam
Therese Winter's "Joy Is Like the Rain." From that milieu
we can sing the St. Louis Jesuits' "You Are Near," Michael
Joncas' "On Eagle's Wings," and Marty Haugen's "Gather
Us In."

Simultaneous with this development was the emergence
of hymnals and service books that provided an avenue into
the mainstream hymnody of Churches outside the Roman
fold. J. S. Paluch's *Missalette* provided an immediate solution as an inexpensive worship aid. World Library birthed
the *People's Mass Book,* whose latest edition appeared in
1984. G.I.A. Publications contributed *Worship,* now in its

third edition. The American Church does not want for print-ed products in its worship.

The vast body of hymnody, the contemporary repertory, the music of the Black and Hispanic churches, the Taizé, mantras—all these point to a scene of vigorous music making whose limits are only the imaginations of the musicians and whose boundaries lie only in the receptivity of the assemblies. Such vigor signals a Church whose breadth of worship welcomes a nineteenth-century hymn and places it beside the latest song from David Haas. The whole of it—music and music maker, instruments and acoustics, the traditional and the modern, all the components of today's music ministry—make rightful claim to the indispensable role of all the faithful in singing the song of the body of Christ.

In liturgical celebrations each person, minister, or layman who has an office to perform, should carry out all and only those parts which pertain to his office by the nature of the rite and the norms of the liturgy.

The Constitution on the Sacred Liturgy, no. 28

Anthropology

MARCHITA B. MAUCK

Anthropologists carry on about stages of development, levels of maturation, passages from one plateau to the next. Liturgists, scholars that they are, enjoy "technospeak" too, and with a gleam in their collective eye, take as their own the anthropological jargon of human life and ritual. Some twenty-five years ago we plunged into the liminality of liturgical reform, awash for a while in the heady lack of constraints, limitations, and expectations that had shaped our experience heretofore. As we look back on those early adolescent experiences we take a deep breath, nervously smile at those around us, and fervently hope they won't remember our particular role in some of our archival material.

From today's vantage point we observe some excruciatingly earnest efforts that in fact have enabled us to ascend a bit closer to wisdom—even though it sometimes seems we are climbing a descending escalator with a piled-high luggage cart in tow! Our mirth is benevolent, reminding us that we are part of an oh-so-human enterprise. The "home movies" of our liturgical infancy and childhood are wonderful! Dams of memories burst, and bonds of shared vulnerability are renewed in the remembering of embarrassing moments. As we look back, surely we can more or less smugly agree with the Virginia Slims ads—"You've come a long way, Baby!" And because we *have* come a long way, we have a much better idea of where we are going.

At the beginning, reformation of the liturgy seemed to call primarily for a rearranging of the furniture. Some of our early preoccupations, the ways we dealt with them, and the direction of contemporary thinking are as follows:

1. *Placement of the altar.* The requirement that the priest face the people was satisfied by the addition of a second altar, often a smaller version of the monumental one up against the back wall. Sometimes the new altar was not a very worthy table, necessitating altar linens that shrouded the whole thing. The priority was to detach the altar from the wall. Today, both placement of the altar *and* its form concern us. Having now detached the altar from the wall, we are looking at ways to express and experience the shared priesthood of the faithful by placing the altar within the assembly. And we are exploring the symbolic form of the altar as image of both sacrifice and banquet. This requires a noble table that is more than domestic dining table and less than ritual sacrificial slab. More- and less-successful solutions have appeared.

2. *Presider's chair.* The one regulation is that the celebrant's chair not be a throne. We are having a hard time letting go of that. Conditioning runs deep. It takes conscious effort to remind ourselves that it is the person, not the furniture, that presides over the assembly. The chair anchors the place from which that person functions. It needs to be movable, since for different liturgical events the position of the presider can change. The chair denotes position, and it affirms that there is order in the assembly. It is not an emblem of rank and distinction.

3. *Introduction of commentator.* In the early days the commentator appeared, to "explain" the scriptural texts people now heard in English for themselves. Thus we kept dual ambos, one for the proclamation of the word and the other for the commentator. Dual ambos made for symmetry in the sanctuary, even though the commentator's lectern was often a beat-up item pirated from the nearest classroom. Today, having mostly gotten rid of both commentators and their lecterns, we are turning to the question of the ambo for the proclamation of the word. What should it look like? Is it a lectern? Is it a shrine for reservation of the Book of Gospels? Is it a defensive barricade to hide the body of the lector? Is it a reading desk? All of the above find expression in churches around the country. Contemporary thinking understands the ambo as a simple reading desk rather than the monumentalizing of a teaching lectern.

4. *Seating of the assembly.* In the early days new church designs favored variations on the fan-shaped arrangement. These tended at times to maintain a spectator or theater model. Guitarists were clustered "up front" to encourage participation of the faithful. The altar rails separating the clergy from the laity, the more sacred area from the less sacred area, began to come down in the dark of night, with only odd-shaped patches of mismatched terrazzo as evidence of the former barrier. An unnoticed consequence of bringing the altar out into the assembly was the unwitting reestablishment of the *effect* of altar rails—modesty panels on the first rows of pews, a new "fence" separating the ministers from the people.

The question of what to do with choirs and other musicians is one of the great contemporary dilemmas. How to have a flexible ritual arena while at the same time providing all the electronic necessities for a variety of microphone and instrumental needs and also keeping the musicians as part of the worshiping assembly is a great challenge. Familiar rectangular and longitudinal axis designs do not lend themselves to adequately satisfying these needs. Of recent date are the appearance of music centrums, significantly large areas designed to accommodate organ consoles, pianos, electronic instruments, ensembles, cantors, and choirs, all in a location for the musicians to lead the community in music and also to participate as members of the worshiping assembly.

5. *Placement of the tabernacle. Environment and Art in Catholic Worship* counsels a location for the tabernacle separate from the Eucharistic worship space in order to distinguish between active celebration of Eucharist and the static presence of the reserved sacrament. Early efforts to relocate the tabernacle off the main axis of the altar (and at the earliest stage, off the main altar itself) led to a migration of the tabernacle to the Mary or Joseph altar flanking the sanctuary. Many people felt this diminished the importance of the reserved sacrament, and they were not pleased. It was clear, visually, that the new location was a "moving aside" of the tabernacle. About ten years ago we thought things would be helped by replacing the old "bullet" tabernacle on the side altar with an up-to-date "microwave" model installed in the wall, thus removing the tabernacle from an altar which should be reserved for the active celebration of Eucharist. This was not a felicitous move. Today our efforts are directed toward designing Eucharistic reservation chapels with tabernacles on pillars or pedestals, standing freely, ever ready for extending the community's worship to those unable to be present on Sunday. We are recover-

ing our tradition of reserving the Eucharist for the sick and additionally providing for the devotional needs of the faithful with a quiet, contemplative place for prayer. New tabernacles are being commissioned from artists. We are recovering the dignity of the reserved Eucharist with beautiful tabernacles and environments for them, and at the same time we are broadening our experience of the purpose of reservation.

6. *Introduction of banners.* The 1960s were the banner years, with glued felt signboards exhorting us, defining terms such as "Easter" or "Joy" or "Lent." No wall escaped, nor did the lecterns or the altar or even the presider's vestments. We haven't entirely learned that wall hangings function best in ways other than as signs, evidenced by the resurgence of old impulses in the RENEW banners that swept the country. But we are moving forward, and in some places very beautiful seasonal tapestries and artist-designed festive fabric pieces are used for processions, outdoor hospitality, and gathering-space decor as well as for honoring the assembly, not just the sanctuary furniture.

7. *Statues.* We know that statues are not supposed to be focal points for the assembly. This does not mean that there is no role for statues in the community's place of worship. Within their appropriate devotional context, we are struggling with allowing images of the saints and other images as well to become occasions for encounters with the holy in our own experience. We are too often content with obtaining a "safe" plaster or hand cast epoxy resin item from a catalog rather than commissioning an artist to create for us an image of Mary that expresses the gentle maternal embrace of her baby or one that images her yes to the will of God. Brought down to eye level and occupying the same

floor plane as we do, art in many forms can confront us with the joys and struggles that bind all God's people through the ages, strengthening us with a renewed awareness of our shared journey.

8. *Dance.* We're doing it, sometimes, and in some places unannounced, with outside dance troupes who disappear in their vans during the recessional hymn. When done well liturgical dance makes of gesture an eloquent and worthy prayer. When not done well it is a disaster.

9. *Baptismal fonts.* Fonts were marble birdbaths locked behind a grill off the foyer. The story of what happened next reveals the ever-greater priority the community places on baptism. First we moved baptism "up front," with a salad bowl on a pedestal. Then we got "living water" for Easter— temporary cascading waterfalls precariously balanced and glued together visually by lava stones, torrents of potted lilies, and varigated caladiums. From there we took a leap of faith and finances and constructed large, prominent, permanent vessels for water. Sometimes we hadn't thought about how to get into them, so our fonts were completed with more-or-less elegant movable stiles for clambering up, into, and out of the tanks. These were the "pious-decor" models— we were certain we needed them but still a bit shaky about how to use them once we got them. There is still some confusion. There are out there in the churches some mighty fine living water, reflecting pool bases for the little enameled holy water stoups that are attached to them.

As the Rite of Christian Initiation of Adults (RCIA) has taken hold, our method of inquiry about fonts has grown more sophisticated. We have discovered that in the early centuries the faithful were baptized in shallow pools of symbolic round, hexagonal, or octagonal shape, and we appropriated these forms with enthusiasm. Our efforts to design fonts of our own times occasionally led to something that was a cross between a shopping-mall fountain and an Italian hotel shower.

Fortunately, we are learning from our mistakes. Today in our celebration of the rites of initiation we are discovering the power of the Pauline imagery of going down into the waters of death with Christ and emerging raised from the dead into resurrection life, new life in Christ, the life of the Christian community. Beautiful, dignified new designs invite the passage through the waters of death into new life, a processional axis from threshhold to Eucharistic table.

*****

With good intentions we have stumbled through twenty-five years, and now we are beginning to see a larger vision beyond the pragmatic moving of furniture. We are beginning to see that our worship places are resources for formation of the spirituality of the Christian people and that there are important links between who we are and what we do as a worshiping assembly.

We are seeing that the ritual sequence of gathering, entering and reentering through baptism and reconciliation, assembling at the Lord's table to be nourished, and then being sent forth, back out into our larger lives, provides a design agenda for our places of worship. Our churches are beginning to look different—but so are we, as we understand and experience what it means to be Church in our time.

The rite of the Mass is to be revised in such a way that the intrinsic nature and purpose of its several parts, as well as the connection between them, may be more clearly manifested, and that devout and active participation by the faithful may be more easily achieved.

The Constitution on the Sacred Liturgy, no. 50

Culture

MARK SEARLE

INTRODUCTION

Mentioning liturgy and culture in the same breath is usually an invitation to take up the topic of the enculturation of liturgy. Or rather, it is usually an invitation to propose a wish list of changes in the name of enculturation: to do for America what Anscar Chupungco has done so well for the Third World. What "liturgies of the future" would we hope to see in this country?

Any such list would surely have to include the development of appropriate liturgical forms for Black Catholics and Hispanic Catholics. It would also surely include finding new ways of speaking to and of God and a reordering of our ministries so that gender would no longer be a criterion for who is or is not called to liturgical leadership.

These are real issues—and issues of participation—where our liturgical practice needs to respond to and incorporate social and cultural changes that "harmonize with its true and authentic spirit."[1] They are issues that deserve to be addressed because they concern values that are consonant with the gospel and are cherished in many sectors of our society, yet are not recognized by the institutional Church.

---

1. The Constitution on the Sacred Liturgy, no. 37.

Having just returned from a year in Europe, week by week attending Mass not only in a different language but in a different style, depending on the country, I have been made aware of how much the Roman liturgy has already been enculturated both in Europe and in America. As long as we remain inside our own culture the liturgy we celebrate, for all that it is in our mother tongue, may seem still to speak with a foreign accent. The effect of traveling overseas, however, has been to make me realize that the liturgy as celebrated in the average American parish church is no longer the Roman liturgy: Catholic certainly, but no longer Roman. Studying the genesis of the reformed Order of Mass has made me recognize that what happens in our churches on Sunday mornings is not so much what the *Consilium* had in mind as something that has come to assume many of the characteristic features of the surrounding culture. Without benefit of preliminary study or special hearings, without any decision by the National Conference of Catholic Bishops, the liturgy has been enculturated. We have made it our own.

It is this unheralded and largely unwitting enculturation that I would like to propose for your reflection: the way active participation has already been Americanized. We begin with some brief remarks about the inevitability of enculturation and its ambivalence and then turn to the term "participation." How is the term used by Americans in ordinary life, and how might this relate to the way it is used in theology and in the Church's documents? I shall conclude with some proposals about what the requirements of our times and of the liturgical tradition of the Church might indicate to be appropriate courses of action.

ENCULTURATION

Surveying the literature on enculturation, whether of the
gospel in general or the liturgy in particular, one cannot but
be impressed by the force of the argument that enculturation is not an option for the Church today but an impera-
tive deriving from the incarnational character of the very
economy of redemption. In God's saving revelation the culture and history of one particular people provided the context in which the saving Word was made flesh. Subsequently,
the same incarnational principle has meant that every culture is called upon to provide in turn the language of faith,
and thus the language of salvation, for believers in whom
that Word continues to be enfleshed from generation to
generation.

Now, there have been numerous occasions in the course
of the history of Christianity when the problem of whether
certain cultural forms could be adopted or dispensed with
was raised explicitly and decided by decree. The Council
of Jerusalem in Acts 15 is only the earliest example. For the
most part however, liturgies evolve in a far less self-conscious
way, as if possessed of a chameleon-like capacity to blend
into the life, manners, and imagination of the participants.
So natural, in fact, and so inevitable is this process that the
issue confronted by Church authorities has usually been not
whether enculturation should be undertaken but whether
it should be approved or stopped. Yet the inevitability of
unconscious cultural assimilation is an issue rarely raised
in the literature.

The liturgy that Paul introduced to the Greek world, for
example, was thoroughly Semitic in character: Its symbols,
language and ritual forms would all have been more or less

familiar in Palestine, more or less alien in Athens. We know that the Council of Jerusalem made some decisions about dietary laws, but who decided to separate the Eucharist from the meal? Or who was responsible for deciding that leadership of the Eucharist should be denied to the prophets and restricted to the *episkopos*? Who decided it was appropriate to introduce perfumed oil into the baptismal liturgy? Who first insisted that the elect should be baptized naked? Who decided how Christ was to be represented in the art of the catacombs?

And so it was for most of Christian history: Ritual development was less a matter of official decision making than of organic growth. Even in a period of supposed rigid fixity such as that which followed Trent, the evolution of the baroque and the roccoco transpired without benefit of anyone's permission, and the neo-Gothic followed them not because a pope decreed it but because it was the cultural mood. Similarly today. Seeing what the Dutch and the Germans and the Italians have done with their liturgy—not so much in their liturgical institutes as in their parishes—makes one realize that in a thousand subtle ways each culture, indeed each parish, makes the liturgy its own.

So what conclusion are we to draw? Should we sit back and let the liturgy evolve? Is it merely our impatience that makes us want major changes introduced at once instead of biding our time and waiting for the effects of cultural confrontation to work themselves out, as they inevitably do? Perhaps, but there is more.

In every age, directly or indirectly, the Church confronts the issue of whether to change with the times and remain relevant to its membership or to resist change and risk becoming a religious museum piece. At least, that is how the dilemma is usually put. There is more at stake, however, than holding onto one's membership: There is the question of identity. Is the Church to retain its identity by changing or by remaining the same? For the identity of the Church is not something fixed and unchanging, untouched by history, but something to be discovered and projected anew in every new historical situation. G. K. Chesterton hit the nail on the head when he wrote: "All conservatism is based upon the fact that if you leave things alone you leave them as they are. But you do not. If you leave a thing alone you leave it to a torrent of change. If you leave a white post alone it will soon be a black post. If you particularly want it to be white you must be always painting it again; that is, you must always be having a revolution." In short, the Church must change in order to remain the same.

I do not wish to suggest that the liturgy exists as some sort of pure white post that then gets sullied by culture. The fact of the matter is that the liturgy does not exist except as celebrated by people of a particular culture, and it is always handed on in some cultural form or other. The reason for reforming the liturgy, and this is the only reason for changing it, is that change occurs anyway. Unexamined change, whether unconscious enculturation or estrangement from popular culture, runs the risk of obscuring the nature of the Church and of the economy of grace. The sole justification for deliberate intervention in this process is to ensure that the liturgy, in this new cultural context, perform the same function and convey the same meanings as it did in the old.

This supposes, of course, that you have the perspicacity to notice that the post is no longer white, that is, that you have something—an ideal or a memory or both—with which to compare it. As the philosopher said, "Whoever it was discovered water, you can be sure it wasn't the fish."

Take, for example, the case of the Catholic liturgy in Nazi Germany. Under the guise of "deconfessionalizing" public life and restricting the Churches to their own sphere, the Nazis had suppressed every form of Church involvement in public and social life: Newspapers had been shut down, Catholic trade unions abolished, Church charitable organizations disbanded, and so forth. The last relic of any kind of public life for the Church and the sole means left to the Church for consolidating and motivating its membership was the liturgy. In 1936 the German bishops, deeply concerned about the impact of National Socialist propaganda, especially on younger Catholics, drew up guidelines for the Catholic youth movement which made the liturgy the primary instrument of pastoral care and which permitted the ideas about Church, tradition, community, and participation being promoted by the liturgical movement to be implemented in special celebrations of the liturgy with young people. It was originally as a counter to Hitler Youth rallies that the restoration of the Easter Vigil to a nighttime celebration was proposed; it was to counter the Nazi mystique of *das deutsche Volk* that a sense of the Church as the community of Christ's body was fostered. Active participation in the liturgy was to act as an antidote to the diabolical mass liturgies of Dr. Goebbels and his Ministry of Propaganda.

This official adoption of the liturgical movement did not sit well with all the German clergy. The Hitler years were marked, for the Catholic Church, by a bitter internal argument over whether the needs of the faithful were better served under these exceptional circumstances by introducing new ideas and new pastoral methods or by sticking to the tried and true: to hellfire preaching, to individualistic administration of the sacraments, and to the traditional devotions to Christ, Mary, and the saints that were so deeply rooted in German Catholic life. So acute did the controversy become that the German episcopate, itself deeply divided, was incapable of dealing with it. The two bishops who had been appointed to the newly formed National Liturgical Commission bypassed the hierarchy of "Greater Germany" and wrote directly to Pope Pius XII to ask him for his position on these matters. Their letter presents a fascinating list of the sort of adaptations that were being put forward regarding celebration of the sacraments, restoration of the Easter Vigil, the use of vernacular hymns at Mass, and so on. The list was already growing familiar, even in 1940. But then the bishops felt compelled to add another item of liturgical adaptation that was not part of the wish list of the liturgical movement but which was already widely implemented in Germany:

> Your Holiness is aware that extreme anti-semitism prevails in Germany, both in word and action. Certainly, believing Catholics strive to follow the line of the Gospel, but it is a fact that, as a result of incessant propaganda, popular feelings among the people, including the clergy, have become sensitive (*empfindlich*). Many good Catholics and even priests find it hard to tolerate the strong Jewish influence (*Einschlag*) on the prayer life of the Church. Such is the state of affairs in fact that certain Old Testament names like Abraham, Isaac, Jacob, Israel, Sarah, etc. arouse great antipathy. As a consequence, many priests, in the nuptial blessing, for example, simply omit these names or mutter the prayers as unintelligibly as possible in order not to give offense or to render odious the sacraments and blessings of the Church. We too have come to the conclusion that such matters as these, in the nuptial blessing and elsewhere, have to be dealt with

without altering the text but by simply omitting them and we would be happy to be assured that this taking into account of popular sensibilities would not be considered to be against the mind of the Church.[2]

Perhaps knowing that his reply would be intercepted by the Nazi government, Pius XII gave a guarded but firm response in which he suggested that some of the proposed reforms were certainly to be encouraged but that others touched, as he put it, "on the relation—which remains always the same whatever events occur or tendencies arise—between the old and new covenant, between the writings of the Old and New Testaments as parts of one and the same diving revelation."[3]

I cite this historical instance to make two points that seem to me to be worthy of our consideration.

First, in the case of Nazi Germany, the liturgical movement was fostering liturgical change not in order to enculturate the liturgy but to create a sense of Catholic identity in the face of a state culture that was actively hostile to Christian values. In this, the German liturgical movement of the thirties was remaining faithful to a feature of the liturgical movement which had characterized it from the beginning. For Guéanger in France in the aftermath of the French revolution, for Pius X in the aftermath of the *Risorgimento,* for our own Virgil Michel in the midst of the Great Depression, for Romano Guardini in Nazi Germany, the whole motivation of the liturgical movement was *counter*cultural. Liturgical renewal had as its original and primary goal not the accommodation of the liturgy to the people but the accom-

2. *Denkschrift der Bischöfe Stohr und Landerdorfer an Papst Pius XII von 2. Juni 1942.* 529.
3. July 25, 1942.

modation of the people to the liturgy, so that when the people were thoroughly imbued with the spirit of the liturgy they would be able to work to change their culture. The true spirit of the liturgy, it was believed, ran counter to the spirit of the age in being communitarian and objective as opposed to individualistic and subjective. Far from bringing it into line with the spirit of the age, the goal of the proposed reforms was to rescue the liturgy from the accommodations to individualism, emotionalism, and worldliness that had already occurred.

Somehow this goal was lost sight of along the way, so that the reforms of Vatican II were promoted more as an accommodation to culture than a call for the conversion and baptism of culture. John XXIII's call for *aggiornamento* drowned out the memory of the earlier call for social regeneration.

Second, the fact that so many German clergy with no interest in reforming the liturgical life of the Church were nonetheless adapting it as they went along to conform to the cultural expectations of the time is a chilling instance of how cultural adaptation occurs without waiting for direction from above or for the sanction of the experts. And note that unlike the changes being promoted by the liturgical movement, this de facto accommodation was so deeply rooted in German Catholicism that the two bishops most closely associated with the liturgical renewal seem to have considered that it was hopeless to try and do anything about it.

It is easy to recognize how cultural accommodation was at work in Germany in the 1930s, but what of America in the 1980s? Precisely because our culture is the framework in and through which we view the world, it is extremely difficult for us to detect our own cultural biases. Because culture consists of the values and horizons we take for granted, we forget that it is there, shaping and distorting the way we see and think and act. That, I suppose, is why we tend to talk, for example, as if the liturgy with which we are familiar in this country were explicable solely in terms of the history of the rites and the decrees of Vatican II. But Notre Dame historian Jay Dolan has recently reminded us that

> in trying to put the past fifty years of American Catholic history in context, it is important to realize that the Second Vatican Council was only one of several major influences on the transformation of American Catholicism. In fact, it is fair to say that World War II had as much influence on the shaping of contemporary American Catholicism as did the Second Vatican Council. Another way of putting this is to state that social and cultural forces were as important as theological developments in transforming American Catholicism.[4]

An entirely innocuous example of unconscious enculturation can be found in the way we conduct the concluding rite of the Mass. The Roman rite never had any tradition of a closing hymn, and its rubrics never provided for a final procession. To this day most European Catholics bring the Mass to an end without apparently feeling the need for a recessional. Yet in the English-speaking world it seems impossible to conclude without a rousing hymn! A less value-neutral example might be the common assumption that we are Catholics because we choose to be rather than because we have been chosen, or the assumption that worship is justi-

4. Jay P. Dolan and others, *Transforming Parish Ministry: Changing Roles of Catholic Clergy, Laity, and Women Religious* (New York: Crossroad, 1989).

We are Catholics because we have been chosen

fied by the sensible psychological boost it gives the worshipers. Precisely because of the importance of such cultural presuppositions, we really ought to stop talking as if all our liturgical practice were simply a more-or-less adequate implementation of Vatican II. We have not merely implemented Vatican II and the postconciliar reforms; we have, as a people, interpreted them. For better or worse our liturgy has become enculturated. We have made it our own, and it mirrors back to us in a thousand miniscule details the strengths and the weaknesses, the beauty and the ugliness, of our collective soul.

If talk of "a thousand miniscule details" seems overstated, consider for a moment how much of our liturgy is actually subject to Roman supervision and thus perhaps to some degree immune to cultural influence. There are the texts, the Lectionary, and the calendar but not a whole lot more. Robert Taft has written about the "soft points" in the structure of the liturgy where ritual excrescences have traditionally tended to appear: the opening rites, the preparation of the gifts, the Communion rite. And indeed, these are the points in the Liturgy of the Mass where in America today the greatest diversity of practice is found. But this hardly begins to describe the wealth of options open to priest and parish for them to make the liturgy their own.

Think of church design, for example. The Vatican has issued no blueprint for a standard church design nor even suggested a preferred style. If there are pews or rows of seats in all our churches, that is not because liturgical law requires it but because our culture does. Or think of liturgical music. The revisers of the Order of Mass intended that there should be fixed chants assigned to the entrance rite and the Communion rite, and that standard ordinaries of the Mass would be everywhere sung in accordance with episcopal directives. Instead we have guitars and folk songs, missalettes and hymnals, and every parish tacks together the musical dimension of its liturgy as it pleases. Or think again of the provision in The General Instruction of the Roman Missal for the priest "to give . . . the people a few directions, words of introduction or conclusion" at various points in the rite. The effect of all this is that the messages actually communicated in the liturgy are dependent as never before on the inspiration and gifts of the presider, the local musicians, and the mindset of the parish. Anyone who has traveled abroad will have been struck, I am sure, by such intangibles as these that make an American parish celebration conspicuously different from that of a slum church in Mexico or a village church in Austria or a small-town basilica in Italy.

Among these intangibles must be counted the things we do not do. One Sunday in July, on a warm and sunny afternoon, we turned off a main road in Yugoslavia and pulled into a quiet hillside village. Its huddle of houses and walled gardens was dominated by the flaking facade of the eighteenth-century village church. Pushing our way inside the front door, we were startled to find the priest seated in the sanctuary in alb and cope with half a dozen altar boys and a choir of fifteen or twenty young women at the back of the church. It was about three-thirty in the afternoon, and these Yugoslav peasants were singing Vespers. How many American parishes sing Vespers on Sunday afternoons in July? The characteristic pattern of our liturgical life is created as much by what we do not do as by what we do. The characteristic ethos of our assemblies is the effect of a thousand minute details uncontrolled and uncontrollable by Rome, details we hardly think of until we encounter a different ethos and know it to be strange and unfamiliar.

I do not mean to suggest that we are not as devout or as committed as are Yugoslavian Catholics, but our affluence does at least mean that we have other things to do with our time. They probably do not need to change their routine because most of the parishioners are off on vacation; not having cars, they do not need a large parking lot, and they are not tempted to skip Vespers and drive to the beach instead. Not living in suburbia, they have not already committed their Sunday afternoons to cleaning out the pool or driving over to the mall or sitting down for a long afternoon with the Sunday edition of the New York Times. That, I think, is what Jay Dolan means when he says that World War II did more to shape contemporary American Catholics than Vatican II. For with World War II came a long period of sustained economic growth, the rise in real income, the spread of the automobile, the flight to the suburbs. With it came also the GI Bill and the expansion of the educated middle class. And from developments such as these came the split, Dolan argues, between the poor black inner-city parish and the wealthy white suburban parish, a split whose healing he sees to be the major pastoral challenge facing the Church in our time.

Enculturation has taken place and it is us. The gospel, after all, is implanted not in institutions but in the people who make up the institutions. We are no longer Italian Americans or German Americans or Irish Americans; we are American Catholics, for the most part white middle-class suburbanites. The hyphenated Catholics are those who have still not made it, who are still not entirely assimilated into the dominant culture: the Hispanic-American Catholics, the Black-American Catholics, the Native-American Catholics, and so on.

PARTICIPATION
Participation in the American Cultural Context

Against that background, one can understand better the ironies that tend to cluster around the term "active participation." It is not a term with a purely liturgical frame of reference.

It is, for example, a term we tend to use a lot in education, where we tell students that their grade will be assessed in part on the basis of "class participation." In other words, they are expected to be present at all times and to make a sincere effort to appear interested and to join in discussions. It also tends to figure in political vocabulary, where "participation" is often synonymous with "voter turnout." However, for those who consider that we are making a mockery of democracy and endangering its future by identifying it with voting once every two years, one of the great critical issues of our time is that of how we are to create a truly participatory democracy, a democracy in which people have some sense of engagement in the processes by which decisions affecting their lives are made.

In a less weighty but nonetheless significant use the term "participation" also means for Americans the act of joining wholeheartedly in social life and social events. It means joining in the fun, being friendly and outgoing, and not being a party pooper. It means being part of a Friday night audience for the *Tonight Show* or being willing to take your chance on *Wheel of Fortune*. It is a term associated with high spirits and high noise levels.

But perhaps the most important feature of participation as we understand it in this country is that it is voluntary. Participation is a high value in our culture, but it is second to the yet higher values of being free *not* to participate and being free to participate on one's own terms. Listening to the radio one morning recently, I heard a perfect illustration of what I mean. An announcement was made about a harvest festival being planned by a local church. Harvest festivals, as anyone knows, are events in which rural communities gather to give thanks to God for a successful harvest. This one, however, was open to all—at six dollars a head. So, from bringing the fruits of the harvest to share or give away in a celebration of gratitude, the format had changed to a pay-as-you-eat meal. Given the number of non-farmers now living in the country, it is perhaps understandable that a community meal might entail some people making financial contributions, but it was the last line of the notice that really struck me: "Take-outs are available." Such are the changing expectations associated with the idea of "participation."

Such, too, I suspect, are the expectations aroused by the term "active participation" in the minds of American Catholics, especially when associated with the term "celebration." Not, unfortunately, participation as in "participatory democracy," but participation as in a classroom or a party: participation on your own terms, participation without responsibility.

This approach to participation manifests itself in many ways, but one struck me with particular force on my return from Europe. American priests preside at the liturgy in a style virtually unknown anywhere else in the world. The air of informality, the use of humor, the casual posture, are unique to the American Church, just as they are characteristic of American newscasters and weather forecasters in comparison with their European counterparts, who seem content to just read the news. There are reasons for this, and they are probably to be found in what some have called the "ideology of intimacy."[5] The ideology of intimacy gives rise to the conviction, for example, that social distance is wrong and that therefore strangers should act as if they were old friends and address each other by their first names, or that public figures should abandon all reserve to air their private lives in public places. The breakdown of traditional forms of community has given us the freedom to which we are accustomed, but it also has its price, and that price is that one lives in a world overwhelmingly populated by strangers. Television, as its name implies, serves both to overcome distance and to maintain it. The people on the TV screen—and the average American is reputed to watch nearly seven hours of TV each day—can enter our homes without threatening our privacy or requiring us to put ourselves out. They look into our eyes and smile and chat away like old familiar friends—from Johnny Carson to the weatherman to your local car dealer. This is the cultural model, it appears, that governs the relationship of the ministers to the assembly. And it is not just the presider. My mother-in-law, a reliable barometer of Catholic sensibilities, says she does not like to receive Communion from lay ministers because they grin at you. She might have said the same about many presiders who grin at you while they are supposed to be speaking to God, but she probably has the good sense to bury her head in her hands! In any case, we need to ask ourselves whether the participation that eye contact is intended to foster is the same kind of participation that is demanded by the nature of the liturgy.

5. The term was coined by Richard Sennet in *The Fall of Public Man* (New York: Knopf, 1977).

Participation in the Catholic Tradition

The term "participation" had a long and honorable history
in Christian theology well before Pius X and Vatican II took
it up. As a philosophical concept, it originated with Plato's
attempt to grapple with the problem of how things could
be the same yet different. His solution was to propose that
different beings participate in being in different ways and — *Plato*
to different degrees.[6] While this was an idea that Christian
theologians used to reflect on the relationship between God
and the various orders of creation, St. Thomas Aquinas used
the term "participation" in the context of his discussion on
the sacraments.

He used the term first to speak about the sanctifying
grace that is signified and communicated in the sacramental liturgies of the Church.[7] What is sanctifying grace? It
is, he said, nothing less than a certain participation in the
life of God, a certain participated likeness of the divine nature. To say that the sacraments cause grace is to say that
the ultimate purpose of the sacramental liturgies of the
Church is to engage, maintain, and strengthen us in the very
life of God. *NB*

We participate or share in that divine life, however, with
all the rest of redeemed humanity. The oneness of God and
of the Spirit of God means that we share this divine life with — *Communio*
one another. We are related to God not as being alone with
the Alone but as forming a new collectivity, one born not
of the will of the flesh nor of human choosing but of God.

The first of this new creation, the one to whom these
words of John's Gospel most directly apply was, of course, *Jesus*

6. See L. B. Puntel, "Participation," *Encyclopedia of Theology*, ed.
Karl Rahner (London, 1975) 1160–63.
7. Summa Th. III, q.62, art. 2.

Jesus, the only Son of God, who humbled himself to participate in our human life so that we might be lifted up to participate in the divine life. In other words, the opportunity to participate in the divine life was opened for us by the Word made flesh, and the human form that participation in the divine life takes has been definitively established for us in the paradigmatic life and obedience unto death of the Son of God. It is through that submission, according to St. Paul, that Jesus was "designated Son of God in power according to the Spirit of holiness by his resurrection from the dead (Rom 1:4). The Spirit of holiness, the Spirit whose dominion in our lives constitutes our participation in the life of God, is the Spirit of Christ, the Spirit whose finality is to transform us as individuals and as a people into the likeness of the crucified and exalted Christ.

 And this leads us to the second context in which St. Thomas used the term "participation." Trying to make sense of a tradition of sacramental theology that had attributed various effects to the sacraments of initiation and orders, St. Thomas made a distinction between grace, which is constituted by our relation to God, and the character given by these sacraments. Grace, as we saw, is a certain participation in the divine life. While many theologians envisioned "character" as some sort of mark on the soul, St. Thomas, with remarkable originality, spoke of the "characters" conferred by baptism, confirmation, and ordination as "certain participations in the priesthood of Christ, flowing from Christ himself,"[8] certain functions or responsibilities for the worship of God in, with, and through Christ. This is what might properly be called the "ecclesial effect" of the sacraments,

8. Ibid., II, q.63, art. 3.

for it implies our responsibility to exercise our priesthood within the body of Christ, which is the Church.

Moreover, these two forms of participation—participation in the very life of God and participation in the priestly work of Christ before the throne of God—are explicitly related to the liturgical rite itself as the signifier, the outward sign, of these signified realities. St. Thomas calls it the "sacrament" (*sacramentum tantum*), but we are not doing violence to his thought to regard the whole ritual performance as the *sacramentum*, the sign which points beyond itself (1) to our taking part in the priestly worship offered by Christ to the Father and (2) beyond that, since that worship implies heart-to-heart union with God, to participation in the very life of God. Our life is a collective life lived toward the Father, through the Son, in the Spirit of holiness.

We have spoken of grace, character, and ritual action, each of which calls for a specific form of participation. If we reverse the order, we can identify the trajectory to be followed in participating in the liturgy.

At the first level, that of sight and sound, of movement and gesture, "active participation" means being engaged in some *appropriate way in the ritual act*. The ritual act is a collective undertaking, so not everyone participates in the same way. There are different roles, and even within the same role there are times for song and times for silence, times to move and times to desist from moving. There are even times when the appropriate mode of participation is to look on in silence.

However, all that is done at this first level is merely the appropriate way for becoming engaged at the second level, that of participating in the priesthood of Christ. Everyone who is baptized has the right and duty to share Christ's priestly work, a work of self-sacrifice as well as of praise, a work of silent obedience to God's word as well as joyful response. There is "a time to weep and a time to laugh, a time to mourn and a time to dance . . . a time to keep silence and a time to speak" (Eccl 3:4, 7). The rite provides for all these moods and integrates them into the worship of God in Christ. So the goal of active participation is achieved not when the faithful cease to be silent spectators and become vociferous singers but when they sing, watch, speak, gesture, with the consciousness that it is all done *in Christ* to the glory of God. We do *not* own the liturgy. It is *not* our work. It is Christ's liturgy and it is our privilege to participate in it. We need to express and foster that awareness in the way we celebrate.

So, participation in the rite is meant to be participation in the priestly work of Jesus Christ, and participation in the priestly work of Jesus Christ is meant to be the expression in human, historical form of the relationship of the Son to the Father as this is constituted by the Holy Spirit.

Such, then, is the meaning of active participation in the liturgy. To participate fully is (1) to engage in the ritual performance in such a way as (2) to join with Christ and with his body, the Church, in the worship that all creation owes to God. This collective union with Christ in heart and mind and body is the means, in turn, whereby (3) we participate in the very life and love of the Trinity. That is what Christians of every age and every culture have always done, and that is our task and privilege in this time and place.

As liturgists, we are responsible for everything to do with level 1, the performance of the rite. The sole criterion we must follow is this: Does everything done at level 1 lead to levels 2 and 3? This is the point at which culture is crucial.

What in our culture can help? And what is inimical to the ritual involvement, to surrender to the work of Christ, to the life we live together with God?

CONCLUSIONS

Let me conclude with a few brief and tentative remarks about the future of participation.

1. *The issue of participation is wider than getting people to join in the singing.* It is commonly said that our culture is characterized by pluralism, individualism, the privatization of religion, and the ideology of intimacy. Of these, the root characteristic is undoubtedly pluralism. Our culture differs from other, older cultures by its lack of homogeneity. This is simply not going to go away. Individualism and the privatization of religion are the ways human beings have been trying to cope with the rise of mass society with its impersonalism and lack of cultural consensus. However, they represent a first and not very successful response: Individualism and privatization are not only bad for liturgy and for religion, they are bad for humanity. Thus, the search for modes of social participation appropriate to postindustrial mass society is something that includes but goes beyond participation in the liturgy to include participation in the broader life of the Church and in the life of society.

2. *The most important cultural change will be the shattering of our stereotypes of God.* A curious paradox. At Vatican II the Catholic Church discovered itself to be a Church not of one culture—ours—but of all the world's cultures.[9]

9. See Karl Rahner's influential essay "Towards a Basic Theological Interpretation of Vatican II" in *Theological Investigations* (n.d.).

Ironically, this was the very time when sociologists and anthropologists were beginning to talk about the homogenization of cultures as the technologies of communications turn the world into the "global village." Peter Berger, in particular, argued that the characteristic problems facing religion in America and in the whole of modern Western society— "secularization, plualization, subjectivization"—would become those of every country and every tradition.[10] As Christians and non-Christians come to terms with pluralism together, one effect will surely be the relativizing, even the shattering, of our images of God. Every image of God is a false image if it fails to point beyond itself to the God beyond images, beyond words, beyond telling, to the God beyond the God of the Christian, beyond the god of patriarchy or the goddess of the feminists to the God who dwells in unapproachable light.

Mystery

3. *The most immediate and most urgent need is to let God be God in our liturgies.* Participation in the liturgy, we saw, was ultimately participation in Christ's relationship to the mystery we call "God." Anything in the liturgy that does not direct us to that end—anything that focuses on togetherness, instruction, entertaining, even participation—is a distraction at best, idolatry at worst. Liturgy is about coming into the presence of the Ultimate, of that which matters most. It is a crime and a heresy to trivialize it as we do. What we need above all is reverence: reverence in speech, movement, posture. As Edward Fisher reminded us years ago:

> Religious educators need to work harder at communicating the idea that the *way* something is done is at the very foun-

10. *The Sacred Canopy: Elements of a Sociological Theory of Religion* (Garden City, N.Y.: Doubleday, 1967).

dation of the religious life. No activity is religious if it lowers life, and none is secular once it lifts life. *How* a thing is done is rock-bottom communication that goes beyond all words and turns an act into one of worship or into a blasphemy.[11]

The most urgent need in our liturgies is to let God be God and to return the focus of our attention away from missalettes and altar servers, away from guitarists and presiders, back to God. And we do that best not by talking about it but by the way our liturgies are conducted.

4. *The aspect of liturgy most urgently in need of reform and most directly within our power to alter is our use of music.* There are areas of our liturgy that have to change: The Order of Mass needs some cleaning up, and rather more profoundly, the whole way ministry is exercised needs to be reformed by a return to the ideals of the gospel. These will surely come eventually, but if we look at the "soft spots" where, since Vatican II, we have too unreflectively adopted our cultural norms, I would think that music is the most important. In the averge American parish music is chosen because the musicians like the tune and the people can sing along easily. Why else would "Spirit of God" have been sung as a recessional last Sunday? I personally believe we will need much stricter control over liturgical music and that we will need, moreover, to develop a style of music and a way of singing that is unique to the Church's liturgy and not part of our car-radio repertoire: a music that *as music* turns us to confront God, in Christ, by the Spirit who sings through us.

5. *We need to broaden our liturgical practice.* To use a football phrase, we do not use the full width of the field when we identify liturgy with the celebration of the Eucharist and

11. "Everybody Steals From God," Communication as Worship (n.d.).

thus identify cultural adaptation with adapting the Eucharist. There may well be room for musical forms and prayer forms and styles of leadership that are all close to our culture in forms of common prayer and celebration but are not so close to the heart of our tradition as is the Eucharist. Whatever happened to morning and evening prayer, to evening devotions and novenas, to festivals and rogation days, to vigils and Benediction? In the past, it was here that there was room for the culture of the liturgy to meet the culture of the age. If we lose these opportunities and focus everything on the Eucharist and sacraments, we may end up being unable to know the difference between the culture of the age and the culture of the liturgy. And that, in the final instance, is what it all boils down to.

When Prosper Guéranger launched the liturgical movement back in the 1830s, in the period following the French Revolution and the Napoleonic era, he did so because he believed that the shape and spirit of the liturgy of his time obscured rather than manifested the true nature of the liturgy and of the Christian life. The liturgical movement was launched by Guéranger, as it was taken up by Pius X and Lambert Beauduin and Virgil Michel and Romano Guardini and many others, as a movement to counter the prevailing currents of the time. They all believed that the liturgy they inherited—with its baroque churches, its polyphonic Masses in operetta style, its individualistic devotionalism, its sacramental pragmatism—was so well adapted to the prevailing culture that its essential ecclesial and Trinitarian structures were obscured. What they hoped to do was restore the liturgy so that it could speak for itself, to adapt the people to the liturgy so that by change of practice they would come to a change of self-understanding and carry this new understanding of self-in-community over into life in the world. I believe that this vision was lost sight of at Vatican II and that the time has come to revive it. The time has come to relaunch the liturgical movement.

Mother Church earnestly desires that all the faithful should be led to that full, conscious, and active participation in liturgical celebrations which is demanded by the very nature of the liturgy, and to which the Christian people, "a chosen race, a royal priesthood, a holy nation, a redeemed people" (1 Pet 2:9, 4–5), have a right and obligation by reason of their baptism."

The Constitution on the Sacred Liturgy, no. 14

Scripture

IRENE NOWELL, O.S.B.

INTRODUCTION

In the last twenty-five years we have grown used to the idea that the assembly is essential for liturgical worship. What are the roots of this concept? What is it within our heritage that convinces us that liturgy is not the business of a few ministers to whom we delegate the job of worship but rather the right and duty of us all?

I would like to go back to the biblical roots, especially the Old Testament roots, of the concept of assembly, specifically assembly for worship. In order to look at the liturgical assembly, however, we must look at community. It is, after all, community that we look for, not merely assembly. Therefore it is necessary to consider what constitutes this group a community at all. So first of all we must look at covenant.

Therefore I am going to sketch a picture of covenant as central, and then I am going to superimpose two overlays: (1) Community is a primary consequence of covenant, and (2) communal worship is a natural and necessary activity of covenant community. Then I will ask one question: So what?

COVENANT AS CENTRAL
Exodus as Central Event

In order to look at covenant we must look at Exodus. The Exodus is the central event for Israel. God's deliverance of a helpless people from slavery in Egypt is the birth of that people. Not only are the people defined as those whom God delivered, God is defined as "the one who brought us out of Egypt." Everything else in Israel's history is measured by the Exodus event.

An integral part of the Exodus event is the covenant making at Sinai.[1] God gives the Exodus event as motivation to Israel to make covenant. In Exodus 19 God says, "You have seen for yourselves how I treated the Egyptians and how I bore you up on eagle wings and brought you here to myself. Therefore, if you hearken to my voice and keep my covenant, you shall be my special possession, dearer to me than all other people, though all the earth is mine" (Exod 19:4-5). The people respond, "Everything the LORD has said we will do" (Exod 19:8).

The Exodus-Sinai event gives identity to this people and identity to their God (cf. Exod 20:2-3; Num 23:21-22; Judg 6:8).[2] Both the people and God will be known for all generations by this event and by the covenant that continues the event.

Looking Backward: Patriarchs and Creation

Since the Exodus is Israel's central event, everything else is read in light of it, both what happened before and what

1. *Pace* von Rad.
2. See Irene Nowell, "An Exodus Approach to Scripture," *Benedictines* 31 (Fall–Winter, 1976) 82–86.

happened after. So let us take a backward look from the Exodus to the patriarchs and creation. The covenant promises of land, descendants, and election are read back from Sinai to the patriarchs. It is Abraham who first makes covenant with God, Abraham who first receives and believes these promises. God, in faithfulness to Abraham, subsequently makes covenant with his descendants at Sinai.

But covenant can be seen even farther back than that. God's covenant with Abraham is a way of reversing the spread of evil and sin in the world, which is described in Genesis 3–11. Abraham and his descendants will become a blessing to all those who have been afflicted with the curse of sin and death, that is, all peoples. Why does God do this? Because of initial commitments to humankind, commitments that root in the very creation of human beings. God creates human beings in the divine image (see Gen 1:26-27). God's own breath gives them life. God spreads the world at the feet of humanity as their delight and responsibility (see Gen 1:28-30; 2:15; cf. Ps 8). God even from the very beginning is bound to human beings with a life-giving bond. Covenant is already implied in creation.

Looking Forward: Land, Law, Leadership

Looking forward from the Exodus-Sinai event to the long period between entrance into the Land of Promise and the Babylonian Exile, we may consider covenant in three aspects: land, law, leadership.

The land is always a covenant partner.[3] This is implied in the creation story. Human beings are linked to the land.

3. See especially Walter Brueggemann, *The Land* (Overtures to Biblical Theology 1; Philadelphia: Fortress, 1977).

The land cannot be fertile without them. "No grass of the field had sprouted because . . . there was no human being to till the soil" (Gen 2:5). Human beings are responsible for the earth (see Gen 1:28-30). Human sin results in devastation of the earth (see Gen 6–8; cf. Gen 3:17-19). Land is always included in the covenant promises to Abraham and his descendants. The Land of Promise is the goal of the Exodus deliverance. God makes a path in the sea for them to escape Egypt; God makes a path in the river for them to enter the land (cf. Josh 3–4; Ps 114:3). It is seen as one event.

The acquisition of the land is God's covenant gift, but it is not won without struggle. As Brueggemann points out, the trouble with the Promised Land is that "it is always full of Canaanites . . . and Canaanites are always more impressive than Israelites."[4] God makes it very clear, however, that the people must not be deluded into thinking that they have won the land by their own power. The author of Deuteronomy continually warns the people not to forget that it was God's power that won the land, and that God gives it to them not because of their own merit but because of fidelity to the covenant promises to Abraham (cf., for example, Deut 8:6–9:6). The Land of Promise is the gift of God.

The prophets, along with Deuteronomy, warn that the land will be lost if the covenant is broken. The land will suffer because of the sin of the people. Jeremiah asks: "Why is the land ravaged, scorched like a wasteland untraversed? The LORD answered: Because they have abandoned my law, which I set before them, and have not followed it or listened to my voice, but followed rather the hardness of their hearts"

4. Ibid. 68.

(Jer 9:11-13). But God also promises a new covenant involving the land: "On that day I will respond . . . ; I will respond to the heavens, and they shall respond to the earth; the earth shall respond to the grain, and wine, and oil, and these shall respond to Jezreel" (Hos 2:23-24). The land is always a covenant partner.

The second element, law, is always a consequence of covenant. The people are bound to God; thus they are bound to intimacy, to unity with God. The center of the law is to be like God (cf. Lev 19:2). The motivation for command after command is to do something because God does (cf. Exod 22:24-26). To be like God is to live as a covenant people, to live human life to the fullest. Human beings, after all, are created in the image of God. Thus the covenant law binds the covenant people to live with the same righteousness and compassion that God lives.[5]

A third focus for covenant is leadership. Israel does not choose leaders like the other nations. God chooses leaders for Israel. This is most evident with the wilderness leaders and the judges (cf. Exod 3:1-12; Deut 31:23; Judg 6:1-40). Even during the monarchy, however, it is God who chooses. God chooses and rejects Saul (see 1 Sam 9:16-17; 10:17-21; 15:28), chooses David (see 1 Sam 16:1-13), and then promises the dynasty to David's descendants forever (see 2 Sam 7:1-17). Perhaps not always a good choice, but God's choice.

Israel's leaders are responsible for and to the covenant. Good leaders protect the covenant. Moses' prayer in the wilderness causes God to repent of the decision to destroy

5. For an insightful discussion of righteousness and compassion along with worship as demands for the covenant community see P. D. Hanson, *The People Called* (San Francisco: Harper & Row, 1986) 70–78.

the people and the covenant at the incident of the golden calf (see Exod 32:11-14). Hezekiah and Josiah in later centuries institute reform and renew the covenant (see 1 Kgs 18:4-6; 23:1-25). Wicked leaders, however, are destructive of covenant. The prophets continually castigate the leaders for the failure of the people to keep the covenant. Leaders are also called to task for their personal failures to keep covenant law—from David, who is parabled by Nathan (see 2 Sam 12:1-6), to Zedekiah, who is condemned by Jeremiah (see Jer 34:12-22).

Land, law, and leadership are bound to the covenant. The possession and care of the land is a covenant matter. All law is covenant law. Leaders are responsible to and for the covenant. Covenant is central.

Crisis: Exile and Return

John Bright says that the sixth-century Babylonian Exile is the "great watershed of Israel's history."[6] It is certainly the major crisis for covenant. The land has been lost. The law is broken. There is no king any more. The question must arise: Has God finally rejected this people? Is the covenant over?

The amazing fact about the period of Exile is the answer to those questions: No, God has not rejected the people. No, the covenant is not over. From the Exile comes a new, revitalized vision of the covenant. The priestly editing of the Pentateuch emphasizes the fidelity of God, especially the fidelity of God to the unbreakable covenant with Abraham. Exilic prophets like Deutero-Isaiah promise a

6. John Bright, *A History of Israel* (Philadelphia: Westminster, 1972) 343.

glorious return to the land, with Jerusalem itself standing as a lookout awaiting the victory procession (see Isa 40:9-11). The return to the land brings a new resolution to keep the Law. Never again exile! Never again a broken covenant! But the return to the Land of Promise is not a return to Paradise. There are struggles for leadership between a hierarchical system and a charismatic vision. There are struggles to maintain independence and possession of the land. There are struggles over appropriate interpretation of the law. Persecution finally leads to a new vision of the fulfillment of the covenant. According to this apocalyptic vision, God's promises cannot be fulfilled within history because history is too corrupt. The kingdom of God, the perfect living of the covenant, will come only after the great catastrophe that ends history. Then the faithful remnant, the true covenant people, will enjoy the benefits of covenant forever.

COMMUNITY AS EFFECT OF COVENANT

The covenant is central. Now we move to the first overlay: Community is the primary effect of covenant. God makes covenant not with individuals but with a people.

Exodus-Sinai

This fact is evident in the central event of Exodus-Sinai. It is the whole people that is delivered from slavery in Egypt. God delivers all of them, even though none of them has power or prestige. God delivers a motley group of nameless slaves who seem to have no right to divine concern. It is this deliverance that gives them a name and makes them a people.

When they arrive at Sinai, the God who has delivered them makes covenant with them. With all of them. At the beginning of the recital in Exodus 19, Moses brings God's word to all the people. God promises that they all will be a special divine possession, that they will—all together—be a holy people, a kingdom of priests. *All the people* answer, "Everything the LORD says, we will do" (Exod 19:8). After the theophany and the giving of the Law the covenant is sealed with *all the people* (see Exod 24:1-11). In a blood rite the blood of the sacrifice is sprinkled both on the altar, which stands for Yahweh, and on the people. Blood is a sign of life. The blood shared is a sign of life shared. Now these people share life not only with one another but also with God. Now they are blood relatives of God. There is also a shared meal, which indicates shared life. Now the community consists of God with the people.

The covenant formula also emphasizes the fact that the covenant is with all the people. God speaks to them in a wedding formula. The husband says to the bride, "I am your husband and you are my wife from this day forward" (cf. Tob 8:11).[7] God says to the people: "I am your God and you are my people forever."

The covenant made at Sinai is a covenant between God and all the people, not between God and the leaders only, not between God and individuals, but between God and all the people. All the people are now a community with God.

Patriarchs and Creation

Reading backward, we come again to the story of the patriarchs. Even though it seems in these stories that God makes

7. See "Contract of Mibtahiah's Third Marriage," *ANET*, 222. Also see Tob 7:11.

covenant with an individual, a careful reading will show us that this is not so. God makes covenant with Abraham, but already in the first conversation promises land not to him but to his descendants (see Gen 12:7). The covenant is with Abraham and the generations to come. There is even a hint in the first conversation that the rest of us will eventually share in this covenant. Abraham is promised that he and his descendants will be a blessing to all nations (see Gen 12:2-3). Already the covenant promise stretches beyond the first covenant community.

Jacob, Abraham's grandson in the story, is named Israel in his struggle with God (or the angel of God) (see Gen 32:23-31). From that point on, it is difficult to know when we are hearing about the individual, Jacob, and when we are hearing about the people, Israel. Or is there a difference? God covenants with all of them. God names them all, according to the folk etymology, "The One Who Struggles with God." Jacob's twelve sons are the twelve tribes of Israel, and we are already a people.

A further step back takes us to the stories of the beginning. Even there individuals fade into community. Genesis 1:26-27 tells us of the creation of *adam,* "human." In the divine image God created them; male and female God created them. Already community. The Genesis 2 story shows us a closer view of human creation. But even there we have one person named "Human" and another named "Mother of All the Living." The author knew this was a story of all of us, not just of two of us.

The progression of sin, too, moves rapidly from a few of us to all of us. The effect of sin is always separation, alienation. The man and woman in the garden are separated from God, from the earth, and from each other; Cain from all of society; the people of the tower from all whose language is different. The final separation is inevitable; the human being will be separated from life. We are indeed doomed to die. Community has been shattered by sin. Thus, by Genesis 12 we are in great need of Abraham, who with his descendants will be a blessing for all nations. All nations are in serious trouble because of sin. In creation and sin we are already community.

Land, Law, Leadership

Turning again to look in the other direction from the Exodus-Sinai event, we consider land, law, and leadership in the light of community. The movement into the land is a further story of community. The covenant made at Sinai is renewed in the settlement by Joshua and the people at Shechem (see Josh 24:1-28). Because the covenant is living, because the bond with God continues, each generation must renew the covenant. Each generation must choose God. The sin described in the Book of Judges begins to happen when Joshua and all his generation are dead (see Judg 2:8-10). The people are in need of yet another covenant renewal. The covenant is not made once and for all; the covenant lives from generation to generation. The covenant must belong to the community.

The possession of the land is a community possession. The land is given to the people, not to individuals. The land is held by the tribe and cannot be alienated from the tribe. In the Jubilee Year all land must revert to the tribe that holds it (see Lev 25:8-22). The land is part of the covenant promise, is even a covenant partner.[8] The land is part of the community bond between God and the people.

8. See Brueggemann, *The Land.*

The leaders are chosen by God to fit the needs of the community. In the early period judges arise to defeat enemies. The enemies have come because God has sold the people to them. Why? Because they have turned to other gods and the covenant is wounded. The people bear the responsibility together.

At the beginning of the monarchy kings are made not only through anointing by a prophet, which signifies the choice of God, but also by the acclaim of the people. Only with Solomon does this community involvement cease. It reappears, however, with Solomon's son. The Judahites choose Rehoboam; the Israelites reject him and choose Jeroboam instead (see 1 Kgs 12:1-20). The community is involved in choosing kings. The kings in turn are responsible for the community, especially for the most helpless— the widow, the orphan, the stranger. Even the king does not escape covenant community. Prophets who arise during the monarchy are also intimately bound to the community. Carroll Stuhlmueller says that "a prophet cannot be born except in community" and must stay within the community. The true prophet is one who dies within the community.[9]

Covenant law is binding on the community. The covenant making, the making of community, imposes obligations on all parties. All parties are obligated to righteousness and compassion.[10] They have responsibilities for one another. God has acted in compassion by delivering them from slavery and by choosing them to be a special people. They must in turn act in compassion toward one another,

9. Carroll Stuhlmueller, *Thirsting for the Lord* (New York: Paulist, 1977) 41, 51–52.
10. Cf. Hanson, 70–78.

and not only to one another—they must have a special care for the stranger and the slave, remembering that God had special care for them when they were strangers and slaves. They must extend the community beyond its natural limits. God pledges righteousness toward them, pledges to keep the covenant in justice. God is just. They in turn must be just. Biblical righteousness, however, is dependent not simply upon norm but upon relationship. Biblical righteousness is always judged by relationship. Each relationship demands different actions, but all actions must be for the good of the other and modeled upon God.[11] The covenant law obligates the covenant people to make community not only with God but with one another.

Exile and Return

The great miracle of the Exile and return is the preservation of the community. The leaders provide the center. Genealogies that connect the community to Abraham and even to Adam are reconstructed. Customs that allow the people to be faithful to the law anywhere become central customs, for example, circumcision, Sabbath, dietary laws. The Scriptures are collected and edited. All these things hold the people together and keep the identity of the covenant community. The great resolution in the return is to preserve a holy community, a holy people, so that they might never again lose the covenant promises.

11. Cf. Elizabeth Achtemeier, "Righteousness," *IDB* 4.80.

COMMUNAL WORSHIP AS RESPONSE TO COVENANT COMMUNITY

Thus covenant is central; community is a primary effect of covenant. This brings us to the second overlay: Communal worship is a natural and necessary response of the covenant community. The people with whom God has made covenant, the people with whom God has made community, have an obligation to worship this God who has deigned to make covenant community with them.[12] God must be the center of their lives. It is God who has over and over demonstrated power to deliver them. It is God who is their model of righteousness and compassion. It is God who loves them and chooses them. Their response must be love and worship, and this love and worship must be a community activity. Anything else is unthinkable.

Both Hebrew words used for the community assembly have a nuance of being called: *Qahal* probably comes from the word *qol*, "voice"; *'edah* is related to *mo'ed*, "meeting, appointed time and place." The two most common Greek words used to translate these terms in the Septuagint are *ekklesia*, related to the verb "to call together"; and *synagoge*, "led together."[13] Thus there is is an implication of community and of covenant, being called together by God.

I would like to look at the worshiping assembly in four aspects: Sabbath, Passover, Day of Atonement, and a brief glance at the psalms. All of these aspects, you will recognize, have a relationship to our own worship.

---

12. Cf. Hanson, 73–75.
13. *TDNT* 2.291–307

Sabbath

The Sabbath day is central to Israel as a covenant community. Both the priestly tradition in Exodus and the prophet Ezekiel identify the Sabbath as the *sign* of the covenant with Yahweh. The Sabbath "is to be the sign between you and me throughout the generations, to show that it is I, the LORD, who make you holy. . . . Between me and the Israelites it is to be an everlasting sign" (Exod 31:13, 17; cf. Ezek 20:12, 20). To fail to keep the Sabbath is to cease to belong to the covenant community (see Exod 31:14; 35:2; Num 15:32-36).[14] Breaking of the Sabbath results in the ultimate separation; breaking of the Sabbath is punishable by death (see Exod 31:14).

The Sabbath is a sign of the people's own deliverance, the Exodus. Because God has delivered them they are free: free to take time, free to gather, free to worship. The Sabbath is also a sign of creation. Because God takes care of the world they are free to leave it to divine concern one day a week. The God of Israel is different from the gods of the Mesopotamian myth, who made humans to work so the gods could rest. The God of Israel rests so that the people can join in divine rest.

Therefore the Sabbath command is rooted in both creation and Exodus. In the Decalogue in Exodus 20 Israel must keep the Sabbath because God rested on the seventh day. In the other version of the Decalogue, in Deuteronomy 5, Israel must keep the Sabbath in order that the slaves (and even the animals) may rest, since they were once slaves in Egypt and God delivered them.

14. Cf. Roland de Vaux, *Ancient Israel: Its Life and Institutions* (New York: McGraw-Hill, 1965) 482.

Thus, keeping the Sabbath is a way of being like God. The Sabbath is a sign of the Law. The Sabbath is a sign of righteousness. The people have a duty to worship the God who has done so much for them. The Sabbath is a sign of compassion. Remembering their own slavery, they allow rest for their workers.

The Sabbath extends even to the other covenant partner, the land. The land has a right to Sabbath too. Every seven years the land, which is the place of rest for the people (cf. Deut 12:9), is allowed its own rest (see Lev 25:1-7). After seven sabbatical years, in the fiftieth year, the Year of Jubilee, the land as covenant partner and sign returns to the tribe whose inheritance it is. God in turn promises to care for the people with divine blessings in that year (see Lev 25:8-22).

Now what does this have to do with assembly, with gathering? Initially, the Sabbath command applied primarily to rest. Eventually however, it developed into a day of communal worship as well. This development probably happened during the Exile, when Sabbath became one of the important ways the community maintained its identity. It seems to be connected to the (very cloudy) beginnings of the synagogue.[15]

After the Exile Leviticus connects the Sabbath command with the Temple: "Keep my sabbaths, and reverence my sanctuary" (19:30). Special sacrifices are prescribed for the Sabbath day: "On the sabbath day you shall offer two unblemished yearling lambs, with their cereal offering, two tenths of an ephah of fine flour mixed with oil, and with their libations. Each sabbath there shall be the sabbath holocaust in addition to the established holocaust and its libation" (Num 28:9-10; cf. Lev 23:38; 2 Chr 2:3; 8:12-13; 31:3).

15. J. Morgenstern, "Sabbath," *IDB* 4. 135–41; cf. de Vaux, 482–83.

Ezekiel has a glorious vision of Sabbath worship: "The prince shall enter, . . . and while the priests offer his holocausts and peace offerings, he shall worship at the threshold of the gate and then leave. . . . The people of the land shall worship before the LORD at the door of this gate on the sabbaths and the new moons" (Ezek 46:2-3).[16]

In the first century of the Common Era, Josephus tells us that the trumpet sounded to inform the people of the beginning and the end of the Sabbath (see *War* 4.9.12). It was a day characterized by joy and celebration (cf. Isa 58:13). The New Testament presumes the Sabbath assembly and gives us evidence of first-century synagogue worship. Jesus enters the synagogue on the Sabbath and takes up the scroll to read Isaiah (see Luke 4:16-21). Acts reports that the words of the prophets and Moses (the Pentateuch) are read Sabbath after Sabbath (see 13:27; 15:21; cf. 17:1-2). Teaching must also have been a common practice. Jesus is reported to have taught in the synagogues on the Sabbath (see Matt 4:23; Mark 1:21-22; 6:21; Luke 4:31).[17]

Thus the Sabbath day, sign of the covenant, is marked by worship of the covenant community, reading of the Scriptures, teaching, and while the Temple stood, by sacrifice.

Passover

The Passover celebration, like the Sabbath, is firmly rooted in the covenant. Unlike the Sabbath, the Passover seems to be an earlier celebration[18] which always presumes community assembly in some form.

16. Ibid.
17. Ibid.
18. There is scholarly disagreement concerning the origins of Passover. Some scholars follow Wellhausen's theory that the initial feast was

The Passover is the memorial of Israel's central event. It is the assembled community's act of remembering that makes God's saving deed of the Exodus present again for each generation. The Deuteronomic legislation for the celebration, which is implanted in the midst of the story in Exodus, instructs the father to answer his questioning son, "This is the Passover sacrifice of the LORD, who passed over the houses of the Israelites in Egypt; when God struck down the Egyptians, *our* houses were spared" (Exod 12:26-27, italics added). In Deuteronomy it is even clearer that the community saved at the sea extends to all generations: "You shall say to your son, '*We* were once slaves of Pharaoh in Egypt, but the LORD brought *us* out of Egypt with a strong hand and wrought before *our* eyes signs and wonders. . . . God brought *us* from there to lead *us* into the land promised on oath to our ancestors and to give it to *us* (Deut 6:21-23, italics added).

The telling of the story in Exodus 12 presumes a family celebration. But the family must gather the neighbors if the group is not large enough. "If a family is too small for a whole lamb, it shall join the nearest household in procuring one and shall share in the lamb in proportion to the number of persons who partake of it" (Exod 12:4). This family setting may reflect the period of the Exile, when family celebration of Passover along with other celebrations designed to maintain community unity was emphasized. But the priestly

simply that of Unleavened Bread, and that the combination of Passover with Unleavened Bread did not occur until the time of Josiah. Others, notably Kraus and Noth, find the Gilgal tradition in the time of Joshua convincing proof that there was already a Passover celebration at a central shrine in the early years in the land. For a summary of the discussion see J. C. Rylaarsdam, "Passover," *IDB* 3.668; and de Vaux, 484–93.

legislation may also reflect the earliest celebration of Passover. The sacrifice of the lamb comes from a pre-Israelite shepherd rite, intended to protect the vulnerable flock in its spring change of pasture. The blood on the post, which once protected a family's flock, now protects the family itself. Passover seems always to have been a family celebration.

In contrast, Deuteronomy emphasizes the centrality of worship at the Temple. Passover becomes one of the three pilgrimage feasts when all the men of the community must assemble "in the place which the LORD chooses." Even the sacrifice of the lamb must take place at the Temple (see Deut 16:1-8; cf. 16:9-16). The New Testament witnesses to the crowds that gathered in Jerusalem to celebrate Passover in the first century. But after the sacrifice of the lambs in the Temple, with all twenty-four divisions of priests in attendance, the meal still took place in family groups. In this period a place was even provided next to the Temple for families to celebrate the Passover when it occurred on the Sabbath, and they were forbidden to travel with their newly sacrificed lamb.[19]

The people thus assemble to make memorial, remembering and making present God's saving action. They make community with God's people past and future; they make community with God's people present. They renew the covenant.

Day of Atonement

The Day of Atonement is a later feast. Two rituals that imply community occur on the Day of Atonement: a sacrifice for the sin of the people and the expulsion of the scapegoat (see

19. Cf. Rylaarsdam.

Lev 16:1-28). The sacrifice consists of a bull, offered by the high priest for his own sinfulness and for that of his house, and a goat, offered for the sin of the people. Blood from both animals is sprinkled on the mercy seat[20] within the holy of holies (the only time during the year when that sacred place was entered). The altar is also purified with blood.

The second ritual involves the scapegoat. The high priest lays hands on the goat, symbolizing identity with the goat. His sins and the sins of the people thus go with the goat when it is driven into the desert, and a new, holy people is created to worship God in the coming year.

The people for their part are to keep the day as a Sabbath of complete rest. They are to hold a sacred assembly and to fast. In addition to the prescribed sacrifices for atonement, they are to offer a holocaust of one bull, one ram, and seven lambs with cereal offerings (see Lev 16:29-31; 23:26-32; Num 29:7-11).

Thus the community, which exists because of the covenant with God and which rejoices together in the blessings of that covenant, also atones together for sins against that covenant.

Psalms

The great majority of psalms are cultic and communal. Hymns by their very nature presume community. It is impossible in biblical worship to praise God alone! The very structure of the hymn calls for at least one other person.

---

20. The mercy seat seems to have been a substitute for the ark of the covenant in the second Temple. It also disappeared, however, since Josephus tells us that there was nothing in the holy of holies in Herod's temple (*War*, 5.5.5). (One wonders how he knows!) See de Vaux, 300–01.

The first part of the hymn is a call to praise—to other worshipers, to all nations, to all creation. Only after the community is assembled are the reasons for praise given.

The royal psalms concern the king, but the king is the representative of the people before God. In the historical psalms, the people pray their community history, the history that celebrates God's saving deeds for them and that mourns their own failures in keeping the covenant. Only the laments seem predominantly individual. Even there, however, the individuality is an illusion. Although in the lament the afflicted individual goes straight to God, there is always a presumption of the community lurking in the wings, ready to join in the thanksgiving celebration when the lament is over.

Thus, Israel's prayerbook also presumes the covenant community gathered for worship. Sabbath, Passover, Day of Atonement, the prayerbook, all assume community assembly.

IMPLICATIONS FOR US AS CHRISTIAN WORSHIPERS

The implications for us as Christian worshipers are many and clear. First of all, the New Testament itself gives witness to the assembly of Christians for worship. In the Acts of the Apostles the disciples, men and women, are gathered together when the Holy Spirit comes upon them (see Acts 2:1; cf. 1:14). In the same book we read that the early Christians are noted for their gathering for prayer and the communal meal (see Acts 2:42-47). Paul even gives instructions so that there may be order in the assembly (see 1 Cor 14:26-40). Those who gather are to speak one at a time and to edify each other.

The Christian assembly is based on the same truth as the Old Testament assembly. Christians are covenanted to God in Christ. The new covenant is sealed in blood and a meal; both are signs of life shared. Christians who share the supper with Christ share also his death, share also his resurrection. They share not only with him but with one another. Their sharing in his life makes them one body with him (see Rom 6:1-11; 12:4-5; 1 Cor 12:12-27; Eph 4:11-12). They gather, therefore, not by choice but of necessity, in order to be whole. When they fail to recognize the body, they die because the source of their life is lost (see 1 Cor 11:17-34).

The covenant community is bound by covenant law. We, too, are required to be like God. We are required to have the compassion of God for one another, God who gave the only Son for love of us (cf. John 3:16). Matthew tells us that it is according to what we have done for one another—even the least—that we will be judged at the end (see Matt 25:31-46). We are required to have the righteousness of God, who keeps the covenant even when we fail. That, too, is judged by community. We must love one another, even our enemies, because the righteous God makes it rain on the just and the unjust (see Matt 5:43-48; cf. Luke 6:35-36). We are to be like God, but the Christian revelation tells us even more. We learn that God too is community, a community of Persons bound by a love so strong that it too is a Person!

Therefore we are bound to worship in love and gratitude. Our worship must be a witness to covenant community; we must worship together. Our new liturgy presumes community.[21] The assembly is an essential part of the wor-

21. See General Instruction of the Roman Missal, no. 7. "Christ is really present in the assembly itself, which is gathered in his name. . . ."

ship, is itself a sign of the presence of Christ. We presume one another in the division of ministries. No one can do this liturgy alone. We celebrate community with the generations of the past as we make memorial of our saving event, as we make Christ present by our remembering. We read the stories of believers from thousands of years ago and recognize them as our own. We sing songs from all over the world, from England and Australia, from this century and centuries past, and we own them as we sing them. We come to God together. We try, at least, to be truly catholic.

But community in worship is not something that we should automatically presume. Community is probably the most countercultural thing we do. Our culture does everything possible to insulate us from one another. We ride in planes and elevators together but alone. We watch TV in silence or speak only to the screen. We drive to work alone by choice. We do our best to be nice to one another at a distance. How easy it is also to worship in the pew together but alone, strangers and spectators.

I am not asking for more informality and easy intimacy. The loss of formal custom and the demand for intimacy has in fact insulated us from one another, because instinctively we defend ourselves against universal intimacy.[22] No, I am asking for community, community bound by covenant. We are not, as someone once said, "candies in the box, separated by the paper" but one body. How do we overcome our immunity to one another? How do we learn to pray as one body? How do we learn the righteousness and compassion demanded of us as one body? How do we make community with ourselves and God?

22. Francis Mannion, "Liturgy and the Present Crisis of Culture," *Worship* 52 (1988) 107–13.

Good liturgy not only demands community, it creates community. I can tell you what the biblical roots of covenant community and the assembly for worship are. I depend on you to help me share in the liturgy that creates it. However, just as the return to the Promised Land was not return to Paradise for the exiles but was marked by struggle and misunderstanding, our efforts for genuine community, for liturgy that is a sign of covenant community, will also be marked often by struggle and pain.

Still, when the final day comes, when the great crowd that no one can count assembles in the new Jerusalem, then God will say to us, "I am your God; you are my people" (cf. Rev 21:1-3). Then we will know how to be truly one, gathered in joy and worship of the God who has called us. "May [Christ] bring us all together to everlasting life" (*The Rule of St. Benedict* 72).

Hence the laity, dedicated as they are to Christ and anointed by the Holy Spirit, are marvelously called and prepared so that even richer fruits of the Spirit may be produced in them. For all their works, prayers and apostolic undertakings, family and married life, daily work, relaxation of mind and body, if they are accomplished in the Spirit—indeed even the hardships of life if patiently borne—all these become spiritual sacrifices acceptable to God through Jesus Christ (cf. Pet 2:5). In the celebration of the Eucharist these may most fittingly be offered to the Father along with the body of the Lord. And so, worshiping everywhere by their holy actions, the laity consecrate the world itself to God.

Dogmatic Constitution on the Church, no. 34

Liturgy

REMBERT G. WEAKLAND, O.S.B.

INTRODUCTION

Before talking about liturgy as a bridge, I would like to preface my main theme with some remarks about the participatory nature of the Church itself in order to contextualize the liturgy within its proper ecclesiological setting.

One result of the reforms of Vatican II that we seldom reflect on yet is of maximum importance centers on our renewed awareness of the importance of baptism. Baptism, in our present consciousness and in our current ecclesiological thinking, has indeed been upgraded. How often today we hear statements that something or other "flows from our baptism" or "is rooted in our baptism." Such statements may refer to rights in the Church or to duties. Most often, however, they refer to participation in the life and mission of the Church. The strong accent on the centrality of baptism comes from our renewed concept of the nature of the Church itself. This has resulted in a deeper probing of the full meaning of the participation of the laity at all levels—in liturgy, in the inner life of the Church, in building the kingdom of God in the world—and has also become the basis for a special call to holiness of every one of the baptized.

It may seem strange that before Vatican II we did not say explicitly that all the baptized share in the mission of the Church. Our ecclesiological model seemed to make the hierarchy and the clergy responsible for that mission; the laity were just to assist them—if and when asked. The emphasis of Vatican II, however, is unequivocal in making the laity full participants in the mission of the Church, especially as it relates to the world. Thus, in the Dogmatic Constitution on the Church, no. 30, the laity are described as having a particular calling and role in participating in the salvific mission of the Church to the world.

The mission of the Church cannot be seen as separate from the Church itself. It is as full participating members in the life of the local faith community, in union with the universal Church, that all the baptized participate in the mission of the Church to the world. In other words, the source and inspiration for such participation comes from the life of faith lived out in the local church. The basis of any liturgical spirituality, then, is founded on the way in which the baptized, as persons and as members of a convenanted faith community, relate their prayer and worship to the whole mission of the Church, both to the creating of its inner communion *(koinonia)* and to its mission to the world.

For a baptized Christian, liturgy cannot be separated from life, nor life from liturgy. In The Constitution on the Sacred Liturgy, nos. 9 and 10, this concept is made clear. One of the most often-quoted lines from this document opens paragraph 10: "The liturgy is the summit toward which the activity of the Church is directed: it is also the fount from which all her power flows." It is no surprise that the same idea is found in the Dogmatic Constitution on the Church:

Hence the laity, dedicated as they are to Christ and anointed by the Holy Spirit, are marvelously called and prepared so that even richer fruits of the Spirit may be produced in them. For all their works, prayers and apostolic undertakings, family and married life, daily work, relaxation of mind and body, if they are accomplished in the Spirit—indeed even the hardships of life if patiently borne—all these become spiritual sacrifices acceptable to God through Jesus Christ (cf. Pet 2:5). In the celebration of the Eucharist these may most fittingly be offered to the Father along with the body of the Lord. And so, worshiping everywhere by their holy actions, the laity consecrate the world itself to God (no. 34).

For these reasons, I would like to wrap my remarks around the image of liturgy as a bridge—in this case one that acts as a conduit that integrates the whole of life. The elements that must be joined together are the altar, the pulpit, the faith community, and the marketplace. I prefer this image to that used in The Constitution on the Sacred Liturgy, no. 10, where the liturgy seems to be perched at the apex of a pyramid. Such a pyramidic image does not do justice to the connecting force of the liturgy. A more vivid image might be a channel of water connecting several lakes—a common phenomenon. It shows that there is a more vital and living aspect to liturgy, one that flows between and among the items to be connected.

The four bridges (or channels) I would like to construct are these: (1) liturgy as a bridge between the transcendent and the human, (2) liturgy as a bridge between the past and the future, (3) liturgy as a bridge between the personal and the communal, and (4) liturgy as a bridge between the sanctuary and the marketplace.

The Bridge Between the Transcendent
and the Human

As baptized believers we can never marvel enough at the mystery of love exemplified in the incarnation. God comes among us; God enters our personal and communal history. Such a revelation goes beyond our human capability of imagining. This mystery and the awe it inspires are intensified when we become aware of the intimate nature of our union with God through the death and resurrection of Jesus Christ and his sending of the Spirit upon us. The union between Christ and his followers, which John describes so eloquently in his Gospel, is one that defies human analogies. The image that Christ himself uses, that he is the vine and we are the branches, tries to give some help to our limited understanding. The early Patristic period preferred the idea that we receive two gifts in baptism: the uncreated gift (*donum increatum*), or God, and the created gift (*donum creatum*), or grace. Grace brings with its presence the very life of God, the uncreated gift.

Just as we cannot fully explain the hypostatic union, so the mixture of the transcendent divine life with our human earthly existence cannot be fully explained. Such a coming together of the divine and human remains a mystery, the result of the divine love for us and the full expression of God's desire to share totally in our human condition. One can enter into this dimension only with faith and a commitment of reciprocal love.

The old way of expressing this concept in the liturgy was through the Latin term *ex opere operato*. Since this phrase could imply in the minds of many some kind of magic (that is, by reciting certain formulas or performing certain acts

God was automatically controlled by humans), it has been used less frequently—even avoided. We have not yet found a phrase to put in its place, one that shows that God's action is essential to the liturgical act, that the transcendent dimension is what distinguishes this liturgical act from any other human moment. We have not recaptured the depth of the meaning of *ex opere operato* insofar as it recognized God's freely given love extended to us in and through the liturgical act.

It would be sad if we had to create a new slogan today: "Keep God in liturgy." Yet we do run the risk of a certain neo-Pelagianism by our intense accentuation of the human. It is God's kingdom, not ours. Liturgy belongs to God in the first place. We recognize this by associating ourselves with the angels and joining them in the "Holy, holy, holy." We cite the company of the saints at the most solemn moment of the Eucharistic Prayer. We must be aware that God is an active, participating partner in every liturgy. The concept of participation must include God.

Some complain that there is a lack of a sense of the transcendent in the revised liturgy and that we tend to neglect a sense of respect and reverence for sacred things as the liturgy requires. There will always be a delicate balance needed between the loving God who reaches out to us and wants to be a part of our lives and a familiarity with God that could result in a lack of reverence. Our God does not want to be a distant God and, thus, pitched a tent among us. Reverence should not keep us, in Jansenistic fashion, from intimacy with such a loving and merciful God.

Since the human is also one of the components of liturgy, we cannot shy away from the consequences of God taking on the human condition. That humanity is thus loved by God and made holy. God comes into our world here and now to sanctify it. The human as sign and symbol and the human as that which God loves and comes to take up into divine life is not to be despised or relegated to unimportance. After the liturgical renewal of Vatican II, the tendency to want to include the best that is human in the liturgy was a good one. Yet we cannot go back to ritual acts that try, through their incomprehensiveness or esoteric qualities, to create an atmosphere of mystery, since they would be artificial and meaningless to us. We must continue to struggle with the mystery of God's transcendent presence in the daily lives of all of us, in the sinful human condition that we bring with us into the liturgical action.

I must admit, however, that the early liturgical scholars—artistic and intuitive people such as Odo Casel—knew that the early Church, probably because of the Neoplatonic influences of those times, was more aware of the mystery of God's action in the liturgy than later generations and tried to recapture its fullness. I would have to admit, too, that we have not yet come to that same fullness in our liturgical renewal in the United States. Perhaps that is because we have not probed deeply enough into the postmodern psychological attitudes toward the transcendent as they have been affected by scientific, humanistic, and secularizing trends.

On a more practical level, what must we do now so that the transcendent is not lost sight of in our liturgical renewal? As an evident observation I might mention the need for better and more uplifting music and art in our prayer and worship. Art has always acted as a vehicle of the divine. That is why only good art has been admitted by the Church into its rites. Music must also uplift. In this regard the Church has had a long and worthwhile experience. The use of cheap and maudlin texts and music cannot lead to the transcendent, cannot assist the believer in that leap of faith that is needed. At this point in history, quality must be sought after.

The present moment seems to be offering a new opportunity for renewal of the art and architecture of our churches. I am pleased to see so many churches redoing their first rearrangements and rethinking the disposition of elements in their sanctuaries. Right after Vatican II most churches changed their altars to allow the celebrant to say Mass facing the people. Not much else was done. Now the experience we have had over these twenty-odd years is bearing fruit; many churches are making more lasting and more reflective changes, which perhaps we were not ready for right after the council. There is more concern for the artistic quality of what is being done and what is being used.

It is also evident that we see the sacred or the transcendent in people as well as in ritual acts. This is fine provided the two are not separated. So, for example, the kiss of peace can become so expanded that it is no longer a sign and totally interrupts the action and meaning of the moment. I, for one, will welcome the day that it is put at the end of the Liturgy of the Word, where a natural break in the action takes place. Perhaps, however, the least reflective of the transcendent are the customs, music, and ceremonies that accompany the wedding rites. There, we seem so often to slip into pure paganism.

Finally, I notice a trend to add superfluous rites and words to the liturgy. The reforms tried to bring some tidiness into the rites; they are again being supercharged with irrelevant and pietistic distractions. I find this happening with confirmations, weddings, and similar celebrations. One easily forgets in the midst of so much going on what is essential to the rite. What must be kept in mind is that the transcendent, the presence of God, must shine through the acts so that they can be easily recognized as something special, something that belongs to this sacred moment.

THE BRIDGE BETWEEN THE PAST AND THE FUTURE

I begin this section with a quote from the Dogmatic Constitution on the Church. (If I quote this document on the nature of the Church more than the expected Constitution on the Sacred Liturgy, it is to show that the renewal of the liturgy through the council cannot be separated from its ecclesiology.) After speaking about the mystical body of Christ, the bishops continue:

> In that body the life of Christ is communicated to those who believe and who, through the sacraments, are united in a hidden and real way to Christ in his passion and glorification. Through baptism we are formed in the likeness of Christ: "For in one Spirit we were all baptized into one body" (1 Cor 12:13). In this sacred rite fellowship in Christ's death and resurrection is symbolized and is brought about: "For we were buried with him by means of baptism into death"; and if "we were united with him in the likeness of his death, we shall be so in the likeness of his resurrection also" (Rom 6:4-5). Really sharing in the body of the Lord in the breaking of the eucharistic bread, we are taken up into communion with him and with one another (Dogmatic Constitution on the Church, no. 7).

"United in a hidden and real way to Christ in his passion and glorification"—one cannot talk about sacraments or about liturgy without immediately mentioning the death and resurrection of Jesus Christ, to which must be added the sending of the Spirit. The Dogmatic Constitution on the Church makes it clear that every sacrament relates to these events as realities that have both a historical dimension and a present effect. Our faith is historically tied in to Jesus Christ and his life and death. Liturgy never can lose this historical tie because it always relates to Jesus Christ and to those events of his life that for us remain salvific. Every sacrament has this historical reference, but it is most clear in baptism and Eucharist, as the Dogmatic Constitution on the Church points out.

At the same time, all liturgy is eschatological. It is impossible for liturgy not to refer to the end times. St. Thomas used words like "foretaste" to bring out this dimension. Liturgy looks forward as well. It anticipates the end times; it says something about how this moment relates to the *eschaton*.

Liturgy is thus an act that is performed in the here and now, but it receives its strength and meaning from the historical events of the life and death of Jesus Christ. It is also an act that belongs to the "between times" as it looks forward to the total fulfillment at the end of time. In this way liturgy is a bridge between the past and the future that takes place in the present, that is, in this worshiping community that God wants to save. We never lose sight of these dimensions in liturgy. We recall the apostles upon which the Church is founded; we remember the saints and the dead. We are linked to our past. At the same time, we look forward to Christ's return in glory, to the fulfillment of the kingdom at the end of time.

These thrusts are most evident in the Eucharist which is clearly related to the Last Supper and to the sacrifice on the cross—the "new covenant," as Jesus himself calls it—

yet which is always seen as the anticipation of the celestial banquet of which it is but an incomplete foretaste.

In our renewal of the Eucharist we have not emphasized enough the aspect of memorial, or anamnesis. Perhaps in the past we Americans have not been very historically conscious. Such attitudes are changing; still, there is much to be done. We must point out to our people that the Eucharist is a real memorial. It must relate to events that took place in time. We cannot have a sacrament now, at this moment in time, that does not receive its inner meaning and effects through the historical act of Jesus Christ. I feel, too, that we have not emphasized enough the role of the Holy Spirit as the creative bond between those events of Jerusalem, the here and now, and the future. Perhaps we would also have to say that our general intercessions or our petitions are often wanting, since they do not have this breadth of vision. We tend to be too parochial.

As I reflect on my pre–Vatican II religious education, on what was taught about the sacraments and about the Eucharist in particular, I cannot remember that it was ever explained to me what a memorial was all about and how intimately related the Mass really was to the acts of Jesus at the Last Supper and to his death and resurrection. Here, too, the early liturgical reformers of the last century had a deeper appreciation of the theology involved. In our catechesis, it is important that we bring these elements together again.

In the liturgy we are related to Christ in his passion and glorification. Our own spirituality, if it is to be true to the liturgy, must take on that characteristic of the dying and rising of the Lord. Every liturgy unites us precisely with Jesus Christ in those crucial salvific acts. We put on Christ—a dying, rising, and glorified Christ—and we carry this Christ with us into our own daily life and work.

How are we to bring about this attitude among our faithful, so that they remember how important it is to "remember"? We must develop a corporate memory that begins with God's love, that finds expression in our salvation through the death and resurrection of Jesus Christ. We must emphasize the importance of the whole of the Eucharistic Prayer and not isolate the words of consecration as if they were separate from the whole memorial. We must place more emphasis on the use of the word "sacrament" to relate to these historical events as they are played out in the here and now; and we must be careful about the broader, less-precise meaning that refers to all aspects of God's action and presence in the world.

Just as we have renewed our Liturgy of the Word so that Scripture is now important both in its proclamation and in its interpretation by the homilist for the worshiping community, so now we must renew our sacramental sense to bring this present liturgical act into contact, through our corporate memory, with the events of the death and glorification of Jesus Christ. A new enrichment of all the participating members will then take place.

The Bridge Between the Personal and the Communal

In so many ways this challenge of the liturgy—namely, acting as the bridge between the personal and the communal—is the hardest and meets the strongest resistance. In some respects, the bridge has an uphill incline! Our piety before Vatican II was highly individualistic and in many ways remains so today. But there is no liturgy that does not involve the whole faith community. The liturgy belongs to the whole Church; it is not and cannot be just individualistic. I have come to use the distinction between private and personal. One could say that the liturgy can never be private, that is, just belonging to me, but is always personal. Personal means that it touches my inner being, that I am converted and changed by it. It would be wrong in our search for the communal aspects of liturgy to neglect this very personal dimension.

Nevertheless, in our day and age here in the United States, it is the communal aspect that is the most difficult to reacquire. That baptism means entering a community of believers is emphasized by the RCIA, but it is not commonly admitted in the Catholic community. That we are a people of God is emphasized by the Dogmatic Constitution of the Church, but that is not yet a part of our consciousness. The liturgy must be the bridge between this needed personal aspect and the communal aspect. One never worships alone. The Church has never, even before Vatican II, admitted that there could be a private Mass. Every sacrament belongs to the whole Church and must be a part of the whole Church.

Immediately after Vatican II, the strong emphasis on the community of faith gathered to worship began to create a sense of community. I still find this process operative in many parishes. We have come a long way in a short time as far as the history of the Church is concerned. Yet there are many whose only affiliation with the Church consists of a hurried Sunday Mass and who do not feel a part of a community, one that speaks of searching for a true communion among its members as it reaches out to the world. There is still much work to be done. At the same time, more effort must be put forth so that the separate communities do not become provincial. Sometimes one fears that the sense of community has become exclusive rather than inclusive, that is, open to the broader Church and the world.

My belief at this moment is that we are fighting a difficult battle because of the general trends of our culture, which lead to an individualistic approach. Liturgy will help to realign the value systems of our people if they continue to be taught what it means to be disciples of Christ. This approach will have to go hand in hand with other didactic methods that help people see that they must be a part of a larger society, with the duties and obligations that belong to such adherence. I do not see visible success for a few decades yet. Going back to the Tridentine usage will not help the situation but will only reinforce the individualistic pietism that the liturgy must of necessity attack.

By working toward a renewal of the RCIA and the values underneath it, we can make some headway in creating a concept of community. By trying to bring all the sacraments and especially weddings into the community, we may accomplish some of this. Nevertheless, I see this road as an arduous one without many visible signs of success for some time to come. Yet, by persistent maintenance of the liturgy in its challenging and natural form, we will slowly come to create in the minds of our people that they *are* a people, truly God's people.

THE BRIDGE BETWEEN THE SANCTUARY AND THE MARKETPLACE

The Old Testament literature is full of denunciations because the cult was empty: Religious inner feelings and convictions did not correspond to the meaning of the cultic action and were visibly absent from the hearts of God's people. There seems to have been a never-ending problem in religion between cult and life, that is, between worship and daily life. Amos is, of course, the most quoted of the prophets to decry this situation. Jesus himself alludes to the problem in his own day and left us sayings that still interrogate our motives profoundly; he makes clear that there must be a change of heart before our sacrifices will be acceptable. From these sayings it is evident that cult and life form a unity. Liturgy is a bridge between our worship of God and our living out of God's commandments.

Liturgy must challenge us. So often we select themes that are pleasing or texts that we like rather than those that truly raise us to a new level of discipleship. In preaching I notice how often I am tempted to take the easy text rather than the challenging one. Most brides and grooms pick the texts from Corinthians about love over the tougher ones.

Liturgy must also encourage us in our daily lives. It gives motivation and reason to our actions. It sustains us when we need signs of God's love and concern. There are times, too, when liturgy frightens us—the parable of the rich man and Lazarus, for example.

In this context, I would like to mention that liturgy compels us to work toward a more just world. The changed attitudes that must result from hearing the liturgical texts and celebrating the sacraments, especially the Eucharist, must find expression in our changed actions toward others, especially those who are least fortunate, and it must help us see the need for a more just society. Liturgy can in this way become, in the best sense of the term, a socio-religious equalizer.

We continue to seek new ways of making sure that liturgy relates to life. The homily is the most important moment in this regard. In fact, it is the place par excellence where the word of God and our daily existence come together. It is the place where liturgy and life meet. We feel deprived if someone preaches without reference to the Scripture texts of the day, without breaking that word for us and making it applicable to our daily lives.

The general intercessions are also an instrument for gathering our current concerns and lifting them up to God in his mercy. At that moment life and liturgy must become one. The intercessions must be concrete, but they must not be a complete and exhaustive list of all the birthdays of distant relatives or a recounting of personal family problems and worries.

Lastly, I would hope that we could all come to understand better the meaning of Eucharist itself and how it must relate to life. The breaking of bread, as the early Church called it, demands a whole new conduct with regard to our love of neighbor as a way of showing our love of God. The renewal of the liturgy of Holy Thursday makes this point clear. The washing of the feet is an example to all of us—it is the fullest meaning of Eucharist spelled out for us with regard to our daily actions.

CONCLUSION

Liturgical participation cannot be separated from full participation in the total life of the Church as it relates to building up the communion of the faithful and their mission to the world. Liturgical participation goes beyond the walls of the church building and the liturgical act itself. It implies a full belonging to the total life and mission that Jesus gave to his Church. Saying yes to the word of God means saying yes to striving to build a more just society. Saying yes to the memorial of Christ's passion and glorification means saying yes to dying each day and rising in our own daily carrying of the cross. Saying yes during the liturgy means saying yes to being a full partner in the mission of the Church, to being a sign, a sacrament to the world. It means bringing the good news of hope and the signs of God's love to a world starving for such a proclamation. Saying yes in the liturgy is saying yes to bringing justice to those who are in bondage and love to all.

Participation, then, means living the gospel fully. It means praising God in the sanctuary but then returning to live out the word of God in our lives. It means participating in the mission entrusted to the Church—to all of us: to be a sign to the world that God's love is everlasting; that God is with us now; that God has truly pitched a tent among us.

Bibliography

A. G. Martimort. "The Assembly," in A. G. Martimort, *The Church at Prayer: Volume I: Principles of the Liturgy* (Collegeville: The Liturgical Press, 1983) 89–112.

S. Marsilli. *"La liturgia culto della Chiesa." Anámnesis* 1 (Turin, 1974) 107–30.

The Mass of the Future. Gerald Ellard (Milwaukee, 1948).

K. Rahner. *"De praesentia Domini in communitate cultus."* S. Schönmetzer, o.c., 330–38.

G. Cingolani. *L'assemblea e la sua partecipazione al sacrificio eucharistico* (Rome, 1967).

Roles in the Liturgical Assembly, trans. M. J. O'Connell (New York, 1981). Papers of the Twenty-third Liturgical Conference at the Saint-Serge Institute in Paris, June 28 to July 1, 1976.

No source is more fruitful for an understanding of active participation than the conciliar and postconciliar documents themselves. *Documents on the Liturgy,* I.C.E.L. (Collegeville: The Liturgical Press, 1982) provides a superb collection of those documents.